FENG SHUI
for Today

FENG SHUI
for Today

Arranging Your Life
for Health & Wealth

by

KWAN LAU

First edition, 1996

Published by Tengu Books
568 Broadway, Suite 705
New York, NY 10012

Book and cover design by D.S. Noble.

Library of Congress Cataloging-in-Publication Data
Lau, Kwan.
   Feng shui for today: arranging your life for health & wealth /
   by Kwan Lau.—1st ed.
          p.   cm.
   Includes bibliographical references.
   ISBN 0-8348-0356-9 (soft)
   1. Feng-shui   I. Title.
BF1779.F4L38 1996
133.3'33—dc20   96-5148
                                                    CIP

CONTENTS

ACKNOWLEDGMENTS

In the preparation of this book I received much generous help and encouragement from friends, and especially from the staff of Weatherhill. I truly appreciate the patience, time, and kindness shown me by David Noble, Steven Feldman, and Martin Fromm in correcting my various grammatical and spelling errors and in giving me other valuable editorial advice. I would like to express my deepest gratitude to Doris Liang, Ray Furse, Charles L. Richard, Dr. John Fong, Prof. Lars Bergland, Fong Chow, my two sisters, and my folks and friends, for their continuous moral support. And finally, I must thank my late grandfather, Lau Baifu (1877–1941), who passed down his knowledge and understanding of this special art to my family.

PART ONE

Feng Shui Fundamentals

ACCORDING TO THE ANCIENT CHINESE, location and orientation in space are of utmost significance. The placement of our residence, workplace, and the objects and possessions with which we surround ourselves can affect our attitudes and even our psyche. Chinese folklore and mythology teach us that such influences shape a person's behavior and outlook toward the positive or negative, the friendly and unfriendly, the harmonious or the hurtful.

1
The art of harmonious arrangement

This book is concerned with the Chinese folk art of arranging objects to enhance harmony and good luck, called *feng shui*. This ancient knowledge enables us to seek peace and new growth through our relationship with the objects around us, positioning them so that people (Man), environment (Earth), and spirit (Heaven) form a harmonious alliance for progress. There are similar ideas within the Western tradition that are sometimes called "geomancy."

The Chinese word *feng* means wind, and *shui* means water. The phrase "wind and water" symbolizes "wind ascending to the top of a mountain" and "water rising to its crest," which in concert orient a person's attitudes and actions toward success. The origins of feng shui are to be found in ancient astronomy, geographical lore, Chinese folk wisdom, Daoist cosmology and philosophy, and the system of divination found in the *Yijing* (the classical Chinese text also known as the *I Ching*, or *Book of Changes*). The ancient Chinese understood such matters well. Their long history and accumulated cultural experience gave them a unique folk tradition and spirituality that accepted and appreciated such knowledge. These special ingredients gave birth to the fundamental feng shui concept that the arrangement of objects in auspicious locations will cause the mysterious heavenly forces to align with people or things on earth, bringing good luck to wise practitioners of this art.

The ancient Chinese also believed that harmony and balance in life come from sources both internal ("Before Heaven," meaning one's natural endowment) and external ("After Heaven," or the changing conditions of one's environment) to the individual, and reasoned that such influences could increase or decrease a person's chances of success in life. However, nothing is ever guaranteed, and readers should not blindly believe in this art form of feng shui as an absolute truth! In reality, it is more like an artistic stage set, providing a person with an enhanced platform upon which to perform the act of "mind over matter" in overcoming daily obstacles. More than anything else, it is meant to create a positive and friendly environment in which a person may live in harmony both at home and at work.

Traditionally, a knowledgeable Chinese feng shui practitioner is also a competent astrologer and an expert in *Yijing* divination, since these three arts are interrelated and share similar roots. The multifaceted art of feng shui integrates all these branches of ancient folk knowledge. It is also important to know that there are different levels of awareness in feng shui; the spiritual and the intellectual must both be present. In selecting a practitioner you should be very careful to choose someone with integrity and high moral standards in order to avoid "bad apples" and thus bad karma. Use your own good instincts and judgment before engaging an expert to advise you; check things out first and observe carefully. As we know, books, including this one, are about theories, thoughts, and methods only. These are the intellectual aspects of feng shui, whereas the equally important spiritual dimension is difficult to demonstrate in words, and harder to perceive. Such aspects are beyond the scope of any book.

The art of feng shui has been practiced in China and other Asian countries for many centuries, and similar practices were known to the ancient Egyptians, Greeks, Romans, Arabs, Indians, and the native populations of North and South America. Do not expect to become an expert overnight. But gaining a little knowledge of these arts, even at the beginner's level, may save you the complications and unnecessary expense of seeking out an expert!

Knowledge of traditional Chinese feng shui (in all of its many different schools) is generally passed from one generation to the next, either through teacher-disciple relationships or family lineages. This is a serious matter, and masters of this art are acutely aware of the need for time-tested selection of correct disciples. A person lacking the proper sensitivity or sensibility cannot be a true heir, but rather merely an informed enthusiast. After all, this art is not meant for everyone. In fact, some masters have died without passing on their knowledge to any successor, simply because an appropriate heir was not available. By the same token, if the master becomes corrupt, then his or her art and practice could become "spiritually disconnected." Such a person could be quite dangerous, to himself and to other people.

Traditional feng shui masters are trained in exterior feng shui as well as the interior feng shui that is the focus of this book. They spend much time traveling through the countryside and through villages and towns, learning how to search out good sites and avoid bad ones. A compass and a stout pair of hiking shoes are good companions on such journeys, while a broad knowledge of feng shui theory, mythology, folk beliefs, geographic forms and features, water sources, prevailing winds, astrology, the Yijing and the different types of site uses (religious, residential, institutional and so on) are essential for enriching field experience of this kind. The interior feng shui we will study here is based upon the same principles and practices, but should be a bit less strenuous!

Readers should know that they do not need to buy a traditional Chinese feng shui compass (Figure 1), since they are both expensive and very confusing even to those who can read Chinese. However, it is interesting and instructive to have a basic idea of their purpose and use. This is because a traditional Chinese compass is both a tool and a portable dictionary, specially designed to provide all kinds of information for the different feng shui schools and their practitioners.

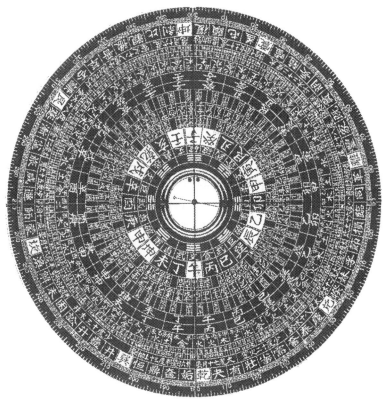

A Chinese feng shui compass is usually made of a very hard and durable wood called boxwood, and is circular in shape, with a diameter ranging from six to eight inches. Sometimes an expensive antique Chinese compass may be made of exotic materials, such as ivory or animal horn, but modern ones are often made of plastic. Imbedded in the center is a small metal compass with a magnetic pointer painted half in red (indicating south) and half in black (indicating north). Surrounding this are concentric bands of feng shui information inscribed in black and red. Traditional Chinese compasses may have six, nine, twelve, or more of these concentric information bands, depending on the school or method of the individual practitioner. Of prime importance are the basic 360 degree demarcations, further arranged into twenty-four directional sectors (generally known as the twenty-four mountains), and the eight cardinal directions, represented by the *bagua*, the eight basic trigrams used in *Yijing* divination. Also included in the information bands and corresponding to the various directional sectors on the compass face are: two ancient Chinese numerical systems, the Ten Heavenly Stems and the Twelve Earthly Branches, used in combination for counting time (hours, days, months, and years); the Five Elements; and the twenty-eight constellations or star lodges recognized by Chinese astrology.

For this book and the Nine Stars method of feng shui analysis that we are going to learn and use, an elaborate traditional compass is unnecessary: an inexpensive, conventional Western-style compass will be fine. This is because all we need are the eight cardinal directions and the various degrees to determine the locations of the different directional sectors. Certain traditional Chinese feng shui schools are sometimes called "Compass Schools," while others are called "Arrangement Schools," but in reality all the schools, whether Compass or Arrangement, must determine the cardinal directions and locations, and they all share similar rules for positioning things such as furnishings and decorations, or architectural elements such as doors and windows. In fact, the names "Compass School" and "Arrangement

School" are themselves new designations created by modern practitioners. The term "Arrangement School" actually refers to practitioners who depend solely on arranging objects and things, often without using a compass or traditionally recognized feng shui methods. This is because learning any of the ancient traditional schools of feng shui requires not only time, patience, understanding, but also gaining the acceptance of a teacher or master, which is not easy. In any case, both types of school exist, and each has its own followers and audience.

2
A brief history of feng shui

FENG SHUI SHARES ITS HISTORICAL DEVELOPMENT with Chinese astrology and divination. It dates back to mythological times, although no reliable historical data tells us when and by whom it was first conceived. However, its close association with the ancient Chinese lodestone compass has led some to think it may have begun around the time the compass was invented, an accomplishment traditionally credited to the Yellow Emperor, the great mythological hero-priest-ruler of ancient China, who is supposed to have lived around 2700 BC. There is no historical proof for this attribution, but one thing is certain: the use of the compass in China is very ancient indeed.

There are few early historical records concerning feng shui, but archeological excavations over the last eighty years in China have occasionally unearthed records dating from the third or fourth centuries BC, with indirect references and fragmentary information related to it. Some scholars think that the knowledge and its practice might have been formulated during the Spring and Autumn or the Warring States periods (770–221 BC), when *Yijing* divination, *yin-yang* theory, and cosmological thought based on the Five Elements were first elaborated and written down. This is possible, because feng shui is very closely related to these systems, especially to the *Yijing*, supposedly compiled around 600 BC by Laozi, the legendary founder of Daoism. But aside from this fragmentary evidence and speculation, there is little reliable information related to feng shui and its early development. Hopefully future excavations in China will shed more light on this matter.

It is not until the early Han dynasty that the name of a well-known scholar and military strategist, Zhang Liang (230?–185 BC), appears in historical records as a feng shui practitioner. According to legend, he received this knowledge from a Daoist priest named Chi Songzi (Red Pine Master). Some say Zhang was also the disciple of another famous adept known as Huang Shigong, or Yellow Stone Master. Both Red Pine and Yellow Stone are traditionally regarded as the founding fathers of feng shui in ancient China (though historians may dispute this, believing feng shui to be a much older tradition).

The Red Pine Master has a special significance for us in this book. He was traditionally held to be the inventor or proponent of the Nine Stars, Eight Entrances, and Bagua Combination Method of feng shui that we will soon discuss and learn. The Nine Stars refer to the seven stars in the constellation known in the West as the Big Dipper (Ursa Major), plus two imaginary star-spirits. The Eight Entrances refer to the eight major points of the compass, and the *bagua* are the eight basic trigrams used in *Yijing* divination (to be discussed in greater detail in Section 11).

During the Three Kingdoms period, another well-known military strategist and genius, Zhu Geliang (181–234 AD), also known as Kongming, appeared in Chinese history. He deployed a tactical formation based on the *bagua* to entrap and destroy his enemies, the army of Wei. Kongming was a great master of military strategy and the art of feng shui and is venerated as a founder of his own feng shui school.

Legend credits these three great masters, Red Pine, Yellow Stone, and Kongming, with laying the foundation for all the other masters of feng shui for the next two thousand years. Some believe that the Yellow Stone Master was also the first person to introduce this art into popular culture: as a result of his efforts, feng shui was no longer merely a treasured secret tool used by the privileged elites and their powerful kings to rule the common people. He began the tradition of selecting talented disciples to spread this knowledge to the public.

During the early Han dynasty (ca. 200 BC) an author known by the name of Qing Niao (Green Bird) wrote a three-volume treatise on feng shui theory called *The Green Bird Classic*. Another famous master, Guo Pu (276–324 AD), appeared during the Western Jin period. He is considered the author of a legendary book on feng shui called *Zang Shu* (The Book of Burials). Unfortunately, only the titles of these early works on feng shui have been passed down to us; the writings themselves are long scattered, lost, or assimilated into other works. Future archeological excavations may unearth portions of these original documents, but today all that remains are later versions, probably dating to the Song dynasty (960–1279 AD). Even modern reprints of these versions are difficult to obtain, and they are written in a form of classical Chinese that is very difficult to understand.

By the seventh century AD, there were numerous writings about the art of feng shui. Again, not many of them have survived: what remains are a handful of titles, and a few later versions by inferior writers. Some think that the paucity of these early written records is due in part to the custom of transmitting information through oral recitation and memorization, as well as the tradition of secret teachings passed in word-codes from masters to disciples, a method that allowed masters to keep their practice and knowledge outside the hands of ordinary scholars, critics, and the ruling elites. Feng shui was an underground art that escaped the attention and reach of mainstream scholars of Chinese art and history, who have generally regarded it as a collection of folklore and superstition. But it has always survived in the hearts and minds of the common people.

The art of feng shui reached its peak during the Tang dynasty (618–906 AD), when many schools and practitioners flourished. Among them were eight very well-known feng shui masters: Yang Junsong, You Yanhan, Li Chunfeng, the Zen master Yi Hang, the Buddhist monk Shima Touto, Liu Baitou, Chen Yahe, and Futu Hong, also a Buddhist. Among these Tang masters, Yang Junsong (ca. 650 AD) had the longest influence and largest following, and through him, as well as the others, many different schools of feng shui have come down to us.

Interest in feng shui and its practice was renewed during the Song dynasty (960–1279 AD), and many more great masters appeared. Among the Song masters, the best known are Wu Aixian (eleventh century AD) and his disciples, Liu Qiwan and You Gongliang. Wu Aixian founded a school called the Thirty-Six Meridians, and wrote a treatise on mountain forms and shapes for use in siting burial grounds and residential buildings. From masters Liu and You came various branches of feng shui practice and interpretation employed throughout the Ming (1368–1643 AD) and Qing (1644–1911 AD) dynasties.

It is said that during the half-millennium spanned by the the Tang and Song dynasties, more than one hundred schools rivaled and contended with each other. They all started with the same basic mythological and cosmological concepts and theories, for which they later developed different interpretations, as each specialized in or concentrated on certain aspects of feng shui. Later some of the schools were absorbed or assimilated into others. The following is a list of the seven main schools recognized and accepted since the Tang and Song dynasties, all of which continue to influence today's practitioners:

1. Nine Stars, Eight Entrances, and Bagua Combination Method
2. Surprising Entrances and Escaping Jai
3. Orthodox Five Elements
4. Double Mountain, Three Harmonies, and Five Elements
5. Bagua and Five Elements
6. Profound Emptiness and Five Elements
7. Hongfen Five Elements

3
Feng shui theory

FENG SHUI THEORY IS COSMOLOGICAL, AND based on abstract Daoist concepts of Man and the Universe. Its goal is the unification of Heaven, Earth, Man, and Matter through the the force known as the Supreme Ultimate (*taiji*).

The ancient Chinese believed that when such unity is established, *qi* (the life force) will flow smoothly in and out of all living and non-living things, and good and productive events will result. Blockage of *qi* will produce the opposite: evil and misfortune.

This theory of the union of Heaven, Earth, and Man is the core of feng shui, from which spring many myths and folk tales. This grand scheme of abstract cosmological thought then intertwined with popular folk beliefs, as the ancient Chinese sought to explain both the visible and invisible forces on earth and the complex and mysterious influence of these forces upon human behavior. Coping with the unpredictable events of life was not their main purpose; what attracted them most was the spiritual quest that served to console them during times of tragedy and hardship. To the ancient Chinese, the integration of man and nature (not the conquest of nature by man) is a true and necessary preparation for the spiritual realm in which man and the universe can be one. Their folk wisdom taught them the capacity to accept the inexplicable and at the same time to establish a concrete foundation in life for peace, hope, and dreams of continuity and prosperity. To the Chinese this attitude is meaningful, comforting, and practical; it is mind over matter, the will to strive onward. Yet it is also rooted in harmony between man and nature, creating a humanistic symphony of a very special kind.

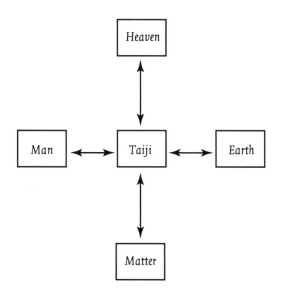

The major aspects of feng shui cosmology are conceived in the following terms:

Heaven is a concept that embraces gods, spirits, stars (in both their astrological and mythological sense); time (including the the cycle of the seasons and its influences); and all manifestations of the visible and the invisible powers and forces of the cosmos. The various techniques of divination, numerology, and other forms of prognostication are also associated with Heaven.

Earth and *Matter* are the terms used to describe all earthly objects and conditions, both visible and invisible. Geographical environments; orientation, location, and position; the Five Elements; the powers and forces of nature; the natural order of balance and contrast; the invisible, interrelated influences of mountains, rivers, trees, rocks, animals, people, houses, objects, and so on—all are part of the realms of Earth and Matter. Also included are elements of the supernatural such as the ghosts and spirits that coexist with man on this earth. The dimensions of the invisible are without time, space, or quantitative limits. The ancient Chinese believed that we all share this world together, be it friendly, harmful, peaceful, or disturbing.

Man signifies the human mind and spirit that must unite with Heaven, Earth, and Matter for harmony and balance to be realized. This can be achieved through the correct establishment of a positive alliance between all the forces in nature, allowing them to flow smoothly and nourish life.

Taiji and qi are terms unique to Chinese cosmology, and are often translated as the Supreme Ultimate and the Life Force. The ancient Chinese believed that the mysterious taiji is the origin of the universe itself, containing the opposing yin and yang forces that in turn are the source of the active, invisible, life-giving force called qi. Because taiji is the ultimate source of this life force, it is through taiji that all things can unite as one.

Qi has no form, shape, or dimension, but through it, all things in the universe manifest themselves in the realms of both the real (visible) and the unreal (invisible). Physical decay is the dissipation of qi, and physical death is its absence. It is a grand abstract concept of the unity and harmony of all things.

Therefore, the Chinese have always thought that people must protect and nourish qi to ensure its continuous growth and flow. Daoism teaches that nourishing qi internally can supplement health and longevity. Similarly, the protection of qi inside a house will lead to peacefulness and harmony. This special concept of qi and its existence penetrate all branches of Chinese art and philosophy, from poetry and painting to acupuncture, meditative practices, herbal medicine, physical exercises, the martial arts, and feng shui.

BECAUSE ALL THINGS IN THE UNIVERSE (living and non-living) possess qi, any room of a house or building, seen as an assemblage of materials, has its own unique qi. Somewhere inside any room is a very sensitive zone or center where its qi is concentrated. This is called the qi center. Just as the qi of a living being needs protection, so the qi center of a room needs attention and nourishment. In other words, a house is a kind of living thing endowed with qi, and it has its own characteristics, orientations, and good and bad associations. The people who live in it share their existence with many other visible and invisible things. Feng shui is a very special and generous art that accepts the fact that other forms of energy—including spirits and ghosts—take their place among the many things that share our existence on this earth.

4
What is a qi center?

For this reason, knowing how to locate the qi center of a space is a very important step. Everything starts from this center, which various teachers may have slightly different ways of finding. Some prefer locating the overall qi center of an entire house in order to determine good or bad locations. Some prefer a room-by-room method, which is a more intimate and detailed approach. All these differing methods have their own followers and audience, and each has its own preferences. In this book, we will use the room-by-room method of spatial analysis.

After locating the qi center, we will learn the Nine Stars, Eight Entrances, and Bagua Combination Method for identifying the various good or bad locations within the space as a whole. This is a very old analytical method, but one that is good for modern design purposes, as it allows flexibility for specific and itemized applications. This traditional method is quite popular in the Far East, where many feng shui practitioners are still using it. This is also my family's tradition, passed down to us from my late grandfather Lau Baifu (1877–1941), who was an expert and practiced it in Hong Kong until the beginning of the World War II. He died two months before the colony was occupied by the Japanese and was spared the sadness and sufferings of the war. We joked about his good timing!

5
Locating the qi center

WITH EXPERIENCE, ONE CAN LOCATE THE QI center visually. One can acquire this experience through practice, just as a good carpenter can tell the uniformity or irregularity of a piece of wood by examining it and sighting along one end. Both visual training and physical examination of the piece of wood are required. This also applies to sighting and locating the qi center of a room.

An on-site visit to inspect and understand all the interior and exterior environments of a space is paramount. This visit can include a visual sighting to locate the qi center, as well as the use of a compass and the Nine Stars method for identifying significant locations. Much depends on the practitioner's experience: some may need to make more than one visit to accomplish all these tasks if it is a complicated space and environment.

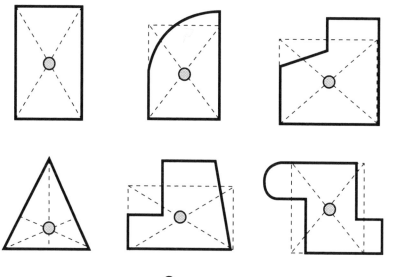

○ Qi Centers

FIGURE 3.

Sighting the qi center can be accomplished by standing in turn at the opposite diagonal corners of a room and visually estimating where each of the opposite diagonal lines bisects it. The common midpoint where these lines cross and meet is the qi center—in other words, the point of convergence of all the major diagonal corner-lines of the room (see *Figure 3*). It takes some practice to acquire this visual skill. Beginners may use tape measures on site, or make drawings in order to fix this point. These methods are useful, but with experience, you should come to the point where you can do without such aids. If the room is irregularly shaped, it must be reconceived as a simple geometric form as shown in *Figure 3*.

This is only an initial approach to locating the qi center. Gifted with long years of practice and rich

A simplified method for locating qi centers.

experience, advanced practitioners and masters use visual sighting in combination with aura-sighting and body-sensing to find the qi center. Once the qi center has been identified, the compass and Nine Stars method may be used for orientation and sector analysis, as we shall see in following sections.

It is important to remember that the ancient Chinese saw the qi center as an abstract point metaphorically equivalent to the physical heart of a living person. It is a spiritual zone inside a room that should be respected, protected, and nourished. When the qi center is weakened, disturbed, or blocked, evil spirits and invisible forces can exert their influence upon the room, disrupting things and causing trouble, unease, and conflict for whoever lives and works there. Here we enter the realm of the supernatural, but this can also serve as a treasure-trove of stimulation for thinking creatively about your life and environment.

6
Yin and Yang

Yin refers to the quiet or inactive areas of a room without doors, entrances, windows, or openings of any kind. Yang represents the active areas of a room, the areas with potential for movement, such as doors, entrances, openings, and windows (Figure 4).

In a bedroom, for example, it is better to place the bed on or near the yin side. The most dangerous location would be underneath windows, where cold drafts may infiltrate to cause illness and headaches. Too much active sunlight or glare is also considered unfriendly, so curtains, blinds, or other devices can tone down the yang side of a room. The goal is to maintain a good balance of

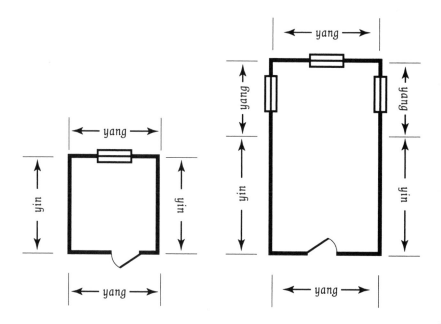

FIGURE 4.

The yin and yang sides of a room.

the active and inactive within a room. Placing a bed close to an active door is also undesirable: such a yang location will have noises, chill air, and the hard edge of the door pointing like a knife-edge at the bed, something we shall discuss later. A bed needs to be placed in a quiet and friendly yin location within the room.

DAOIST COSMOLOGICAL THOUGHT CLASSIFIES all things in the universe into components of five basic elements: metal, wood, water, fire, and earth. These can complement as well as contrast with one another (see Figure 5). Each object in a room is a composite of one or more of these elements, and can, therefore, be arranged to accom-

7

The Five Elements

29

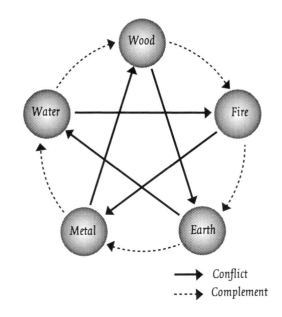

→ Conflict
----→ Complement

plish certain purposes in feng shui. Things can be placed for or against their elements, causing them to neutralize, balance, or compensate for each other and thus indirectly affect the attitudes of the person living or working there.

It is good to place objects where they complement each other and enhance harmony. For example, according to Five Elements theory, it is unwise to place wood or wooden objects next to a stove, since metal conflicts with wood. A wooden chair placed directly next to a metal stove will create conflicts and a fire hazard. However, since metal and water are complementary, it is good to place a water source (a sink or water basin) between the wooden chair and the metal stove. A stove also has its fire element, which is at odds with water, but this particular fire element is contained within metal, separating the fire from direct contact with the water and neutralizing the danger. The fire element of the stove can also be addressed by using ceramic pots and earthenware for cooking purposes, since the elements of fire and earth are complementary.

It is interesting to note that a modern stove or oven, which in feng shui terms is fire contained within metal, is inherently in conflict with itself. The ancient Chinese used earthen or brick stoves, and also preferred earthenware or ceramic pots to metal ones for cooking. In a modern Chinese kitchen, equipped like Western ones with metal stoves and ovens and all kinds of metal cooking utensils, it is very popular to set up a shrine to the "kitchen god." This is an invitation to him to take up residence in this important area, serve as its guardian and protector, and take benevolent charge of all the busy and potentially dangerous activities that take place here.

8

The mythology of the Four Directions

THE ANCIENT CHINESE WERE AGRICULTURAL people, with great respect, fear, and concern for the directions of forces and events that touched their lives. These included sunrise (east), sunset (west), cold winds (north), and warm sunlight (south). Also affecting them were non-seasonal winds and other influences coming from the other quadrants (NE, NW, SE, and SW). The Five Elements we have just discussed were also linked to the points of the compass: north is the domain of water, south of fire, east of wood, and west of metal. Earth occupies the center, surrounded by all the other directions and elements.

Over the course of centuries, a vast body of mythology and folklore has grown up around the

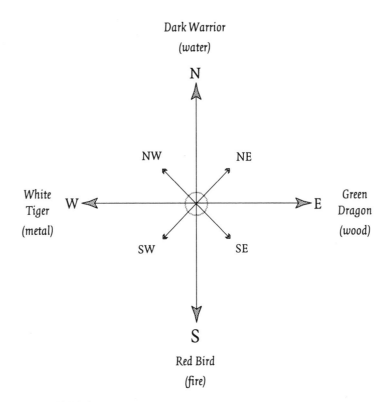

Dark Warrior
(water)

N

NW · NE

White
Tiger · W · E · Green
Dragon
(metal) · *(wood)*

SW · SE

S

Red Bird
(fire)

subject of the four cardinal directions and the cosmological phenomena associated with them (Figure 6).

North. This direction is home to the Dark Warrior, Zhen Wu, who wears a dark purple robe and has long, flowing, jet-black hair. The north symbolizes the yin aspect of things, and water is its element.

Zhen Wu is the Lord of the North and the God of Winter. He occupies the central and most prestigious throne of the night sky, the North Star, around which all the constellations and stars revolve through the four seasons. He is the symbol of justice and wisdom in the night sky, pointing the position of the true north. The Dark Warrior has two wise and loyal disciples, the Snake (symbol of fertility) and the Turtle (symbol of longevity). He is the noble magistrate and the supreme commander of all the stars in his night kingdom. He oversees the cold and chilly northern winter winds that sweep down across the Mongolian plains to freeze and stop all growing activities and cause sickness and misery to people. He also has the ultimate power to drive all the wild and ferocious animals and creatures into hiding or hibernation. He is also, however, the good king who ends the winter with the advent of spring and its regeneration of agriculture.

In feng shui, no openings of any kind are welcome in the north wall of a house. It is better to have a solid heavy wall facing the north, and to place entrances and windows facing south to receive the warm southern sunlight and to neutralize the uncompromising cold air from the north. Frequent ice and snow accumulations in winter are another reason for not orienting the the main entrance of a house to the north. Inside a house, protected by the solid exterior walls, a northern doorway into a room or bedroom is acceptable. As for northern skylights, it is better to have them mounted on a sloping roof or at an angle, not confronting the Dark Warrior head on! Those who want to add some visual warmth to the interior north wall of a house can hang a red, orange, or warmly colored painting or wall decoration to neutralize this chilly location. A warm fireplace on the north wall is also fine.

South. This is the domain of the Red Bird, or Phoenix, also known as the Fire Bird. In Chinese folklore, the Phoenix symbolizes the female gender. But in feng shui it represents the *yang* force, summer, warmth, and the sunny southern direction, and its element is fire. Farmers in China welcome the warm sun to grow crops for a good harvest in the fall; at the same time, they are fearful of the Red Bird because excessive sunlight can cause droughts and damage their crops and land.

In both exterior and interior feng shui, south is the most auspicious direction. Traditional Chinese walled cities, temples, and other important structures were usually oriented to face the south. The Forbidden City in Beijing was built on a precise north-south axis, with all its major halls facing south. A huge wall was built to encircle the entire complex, with its main gates opening to the south, and artificial hills were placed on its northern side to avert evil influences from that direction.

East. The Green Dragon represents the east and is also the symbol of spring, when all of nature starts to wake up and grow. The dragon is a majestic and auspicious animal in Chinese folklore. He represents the emperor and also symbolizes the male gender in Chinese culture. The element of the Green Dragon is wood, complementary to fire but in conflict with earth and metal. In exterior feng shui, a mountain range with ridges is called a "dragon." In interior feng shui, a solid wall or a tall screen embracing a chair or a table placed in a special location is sometimes considered in a similar manner, and seen as warding off unfriendly elements.

In exterior feng shui, if there is a small mountain or hill behind a house, it is thought beneficial to have a stream or a small river passing by on the east side to nourish the site. And the ground at the east side of the house (symbolized by the Green Dragon) should be slightly higher than the ground on the west side (symbolized by the White Tiger) because, according to Chinese mythology, the dragon is an imperial symbol and should command a higher place. Sometimes a sculpture or painting of a Chinese dragon on the interior east wall of a house can scare away evil spirits or overcome an undesirable view, such as a distant smoke stack, a large object with pointed edges, a dead tree trunk, or a cemetery.

West. This is the domain of the White Tiger, whose element is metal. This brave tiger represents autumn and is complementary to water, but in conflict with wood and fire. Therefore, water is good for the west. Water represents *yin*, and therefore fertility, prosperity, wealth, and growth. In addition, water has a very special effect in nourishing the qi of any space. Things related to water such as a lake, a pond, a river or stream, an aquarium with goldfish or tropical fish, water plants, a vase with greens and flowers, or a vase containing water are also beneficial for the westerly direction. In Chinese folklore, the tiger is also a *yang* or male symbol that complements the *yin* water symbol. In Chinese mythology the tiger is a noble animal who protects the heavenly gates to the Western Paradise, and is a faithful disciple of the Buddhist saints called *lohan*, serving them by warding off evil spirits.

In modern feng shui practice, water placed at the west side of a room means money and wealth. But some also consider this direction to represent fertility, love, and romance, because water nourishes such events and relationships. Therefore, the west wall, and sometimes the northwestern corner of a bedroom, is a very popular location for arrangements involving water. In temples and monasteries, altars and shrines are usually arranged facing west. This is because the west is the direction of the Western Paradise, where all the Chinese gods reside. In Daoism, the west is also the garden of the Queen Mother of the West, Si Huangmu.

9
The Nine Stars and their significance

NOW THAT WE HAVE VISITED EACH OF THE Four Directions, we must turn to the Big Dipper, which points throughout the seasons to the majestic North Star, throne of Zhen Wu, the Dark Warrior (Figure 7). For many centuries the North Star, also known in the West as Polaris, has provided guidance for travelers and seafarers, showing them the direction of true north since about 1000 BC. It will continue to do so until around 4000 AD, when it will be succeeded by Vega. Zhen Wu's long imperial reign over the northern position of the night sky would certainly be the envy of any earthly dynasty!

A whole school of feng shui is devoted to the Big Dipper because of its relationship to the North Star. This school of feng shui is the Nine Stars, Eight Entrances, and Bagua Combination Method mentioned earlier. We are going to learn how to use it for our room by room analysis of good and bad sectors.

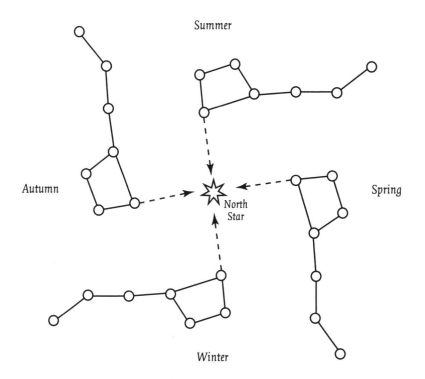

Summer

Autumn

Spring

★ North
Star

Winter

FIGURE 7.

The Big Dipper points to
the North Star through-
out the Four Seasons

The Big Dipper in the night sky has only seven stars. But in feng shui (as in Chinese astrology and divination), two imaginary stars known as star-spirits are added to them to represent the two main aspects of an *Yijing* oracle, indicating good or bad omens. The seven visible stars are numbered and named as follows: 1) Life and Growth, 2) Heavenly Healing, 3) Disaster, 4) Six Conflicts, 5) Five Ghosts, 6) Continuity, and 7) Death. To these seven visible stars are added the two imaginary star-spirits: 8) The Left Assistant, and 9) The Right Assistant, both of which are assigned to the

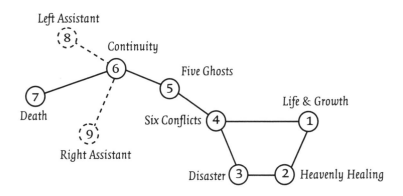

Left Assistant

⟨8⟩

Continuity

⑥ *Five Ghosts*

⑦ ⑤

Death *Life & Growth*

⟨9⟩ *Six Conflicts* ④ ①

Right Assistant

Disaster ③ ② *Heavenly Healing*

FIGURE 8.

The Nine Stars in the Big Dipper.

star Continuity, making a formation of Nine Stars altogether (*Figure 8*).

The Nine Stars represent positive or negative spatial orientations, and are fundamental to the feng shui analysis of a site. The following is a description of the characteristics associated with each of the Nine Stars (We shall see in section 11 how to use this information in a site analysis).

1) *Life and Growth* (positive). Good for all activities, and for bedrooms, living rooms, and kitchens.

2) *Heavenly Healing* (positive). Good for dining rooms, kitchens, bedrooms, conversation nooks, and other areas of frequent human activity.

3) *Disaster* (negative). A bad location for human activity. It is wise to place a good luck object to dissolve or neutralize the influence of this bad location. For this purpose, any of the following can be used effectively: a strong sculpture such as the statue of a lion, tiger, or dragon; a small fountain; a fish bowl or aquarium; a large vase of water with green plants; a cactus plant (with thorns to ward off bad things); or a benevolent religious image.

4) *Six Conflicts* (negative). Never situate a kitchen, dining table, or a family room in this tricky and treacherous location! Nor is it good for bedrooms, living rooms, or conference areas, unless the feng shui practitioner knows ways to ameliorate the negative influences. Book cases, televisions, VCRs, sound systems, and decorative objects may be placed here, but not sofas, desks, or work tables.

5) *Five Ghosts* (negative). This location is also troublesome, especially for daily activities; it is also a poor location for a bedroom. Placing furniture and other objects here is fine, as long as they do not serve as focal points for social or business gatherings. The Five Ghosts location can actually be turned to your advantage if you know how to use it well. For example, with proper arrangement, this tricky spot can put an adversary in a bad position during negotiations. But do not try this if you prefer peace and happiness, for it is a two-edged sword. The owner of a casino or gambling-house would love to place all the gambling tables here to increase his odds of separating his patrons from their money; this sector is a professional gambler's dream or nightmare, depending on whether he is clever enough to manipulate the Five Ghosts into sending the money his way.

6) *Continuity* (positive). This location is good for human activity, for bedrooms, dining areas, living rooms, workrooms, and so on. In general, Continuity is a friendly area in which to arrange things, and it is supported by the Left and Right Assistants.

7) *Death* (negative). This is a very bad location for human activity. Never position a kitchen,

dining area, boardroom, master bedroom, garage, or any other activity space here. This location is safe for storage shelves and racks, books, sound systems, closets, and minor furniture or decorations. Never put a bar, a computer workstation, a playroom, or a pet's house here. To overcome the evil influences of this location, you may position here a religious image, a large floor- or wall-mounted lamp, a thorny cactus plant (but not flowers or greenery), a string of three, five, or seven antique Chinese coins tied with red silk cords, or other good luck charms and talismans that will be discussed later (and are included in this book).

8) and 9) *The Left and Right Assistants*: These imaginary stars accompany Continuity and help it to absorb other invisible influences. They are not assigned positive or negative locations, and are neutral, except in representing the Yijing trigrams. Therefore, they are generally considered good guys, so to speak. Detailed discussion of the Yijing, a very complex system for divination and fortune-telling, lies outside the scope of this book. However, our Nine Stars Method incorporates some elements of the Yijing into its spatial analysis, as we shall see in the next section.

10
Locating entrances

BEFORE WE PROCEED WITH A NINE STARS analysis of a room or space, we must first determine the orientation of the main entrance or entrances of the structure we wish to analyze. Let's try a simple spatial analysis of this kind, locating the entrances for the the ground-floor rooms of a simple apartment or house (*Figure 9*).

The ground floor of this residence has three large rooms, with a stairway leading up to the

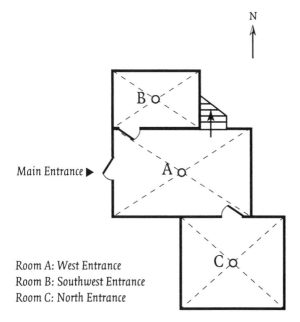

N

Main Entrance ▶

B

A

C

Room A: West Entrance
Room B: Southwest Entrance
Room C: North Entrance

second floor or down to the basement. Of course, there are windows and a back door in this house, but in doing spatial analysis, we do not consider windows, secondary doors, or stairs: simply make a schematic diagram of the space to represent main entrances and qi centers as shown here. This is because windows, stairs, back doors, and so forth belong to more complex feng shui arrangements; here we are dealing strictly with the orientation of main entrances and the identification of good and bad orientations. The example shown here has three rooms: A, B, and C. The main entrance from outside is in the west wall of Room A. Room B has a southwest entrance and Room C has a north entrance.

FIGURE 9

Simplified floor plan of a structure, showing entrances and qi centers, but not windows.

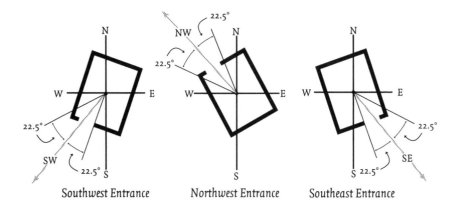

Southwest Entrance   Northwest Entrance   Southeast Entrance

FIGURE 10

Entrances for structures
with variant axes.

For an apartment or a house the main entrance is the front door. If a site has more than one entrance, such as in a store or restaurant, consider the most frequently used entrance to be the main entrance. For an interior space with two or more doors, such as a master bedroom, a large open office space, or a boardroom, select the one closest to the main entrance of the entire building, or the one which sees the most activity and traffic. Again, secondary doors, openings, or entrances are ignored in performing a basic spatial analysis.

The example given in Figure 9 is a relatively easy one, since the structure is precisely oriented on a north-south axis. This is not always the case, and we must learn to deal with structures whose siting is more complex. Figure 10 shows examples of structures oriented along variant axes, and gives the orientation of their main entrances based on the principles we have discussed. The wall of a room may have an entrance at one of three generalized locations, that is, center, left, or right. But whatever its position, it can be seen as being oriented toward one of the eight cardinal compass points. Note that in feng shui each of the eight cardinal directions is considered to include all other minor orientations within its domain of 45° (22.5° on either side of its directional axis).

We have spent this much time on determining the orientation of the main entrance because, along with locating the qi center, this is the most fundamental step in feng shui spatial analysis. Now that this orientation has been correctly established, we can move on to learn the Nine Stars method for determining the positive and negative sectors for the space in question.

11
Spatial analysis using the Nine Stars method

IN MAKING A NINE STARS ANALYSIS OF A SPACE, we must first key the seven visible stars to the eight cardinal points of the compass and then superimpose the resulting matrix over the qi center of the space we wish to analyze. This may sound complicated, but it is not. Figure 11 illustrates this process, applying the stars to a simple structure with its main entrance oriented to the south. As you can see, the southern point of the compass is occupied by the main entrance of the structure; the remaining seven compass points are assigned to the seven visible stars, and take on their attributes. In other words, for this south-facing structure, the northwest sector is ruled by the Death star and is therefore a very negative sector; the east sector, ruled by the star Life and Growth, is a positive one; and so on.

Of course, not all structures have a southern main entrance like the one in Figure 11. In fact, as we have seen earlier, an entrance may be oriented

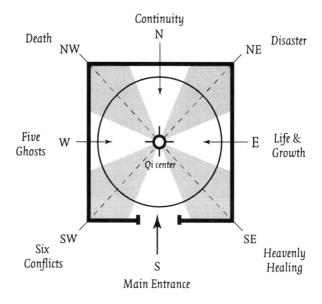

Continuity

Death   N   Disaster
    NW   NE

Five   W   →   ⊙   ←   E   Life &
Ghosts   Qi center   Growth

    SW   SE
Six   Heavenly
Conflicts   S   Healing

Main Entrance

FIGURE 11.

Directional matrix of
the seven visible stars
applied to a room with
a southern entrance.

towards any one of the eight cardinal points of the compass, and depending upon this orientation, the matrix of the stars will be different as well.

Figure 12 is a comprehensive chart of the star matrix for each possible entrance location. This chart is a graphic summary of the traditional feng shui coded word-poems passed on from teachers to disciples since ancient times. Note that the correspondence of each star to a compass point is different for each of the eight entrance locations.

Let's use an example to see how this chart should be read. Say we have a structure whose entrance faces north. Looking at Figure 12, we can see that the star matrix for this entrance assigns the star Life and Growth to the southeast sector, Healing to the east, Disaster to the west, Six Conflicts to the northwest, Five Ghosts to the

EIGHT ENTRANCES	1 Growth	2 Healing	3 Disaster	4 Conflicts	5 Ghosts	6 Continuity	7 Death
North	SE	E	W	NW	NE	S	SW
Northeast	SW	NW	S	E	N	W	SE
East	S	N	SW	NE	NW	SE	W
Southeast	N	S	NW	W	SW	E	NE
South	E	SE	NE	SW	W	N	NW
Southwest	NE	W	E	SE	S	NW	N
West	NW	SW	N	SE	S	NE	E
Northwest	W	NE	SE	N	E	SW	S
INFLUENCE	good	good	bad	bad	tricky	good	bad

FIGURE 12.

The Eight Entrances and their corresponding star matrices.

northeast, Continuity to the south, and Death to the southwest. Along the bottom of the chart are the influences, good or bad, exerted by each of these stars. Thus we see that for a structure with a north entrance, the southwest sector, ruled by Death, is a particularly bad direction, while the southeast, occupied by Life and Growth, is auspicious. Figure 13 gives a graphic representation of the star matrix for a structure of this kind. Compare it to the matrix shown earlier in Figure 11 for a south-facing structure, where Death is to the northwest and Life and Growth rules the east, and you can begin to see how the orientation of the entrance of a structure alters the entire matrix of stars associated with it, and thus changes the

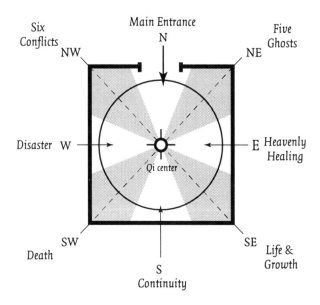

Six Conflicts
NW

Main Entrance
N

Five Ghosts
NE

Disaster W

Qi center

E Heavenly Healing

SW
Death

SE
Life & Growth

S
Continuity

FIGURE 13.

Star matrix for a structure with a northern entrance

positive or negative values of each of the eight cardinal directions. With this, we have completed our study of the fundamentals of spatial analysis using the Nine Stars method.

However, there is more to the Nine Stars Method than this. As you may recall, the full name of this school is the Nine Stars, Eight Entrances, and Bagua Combination Method. Now that we have covered the Nine Stars and the Eight Entrances, it is time to learn something about the *bagua*, or Eight Trigrams.

The *bagua* are the building blocks of the Yijing oracles, an ancient Chinese system of divination set forth in the classical text called the Yijing. Each of these symbols is composed of three lines, which is why it is called a trigram. Each line in the trigram represents either *yang* (a continuous line) or *yin* (a broken line). By alternating all the possible combi-

ENTRANCE	BAGUA	NAME	NATURAL FORCE	FIVE ELEMENTS	BENEFICIARY
N	☵	Kan	Water	Water	young man or adult son
NE	☶	Gen	Mountain	Earth	young boy or youngest son
E	☳	Zhen	Thunder	Wood	mature male or eldest son
SE	☴	Xun	Wind	Wood	mature female or eldest daughter
S	☲	Li	Fire	Fire	young lady or adult daughter
SW	☷	Kun	Earth	Earth	older woman or mother
W	☱	Dui	Wetland	Metal	young girl or youngest daughter
NW	☰	Qian	Heaven	Metal	older man or father

FIGURE 14.

The Eight Entrances with the Eight Trigrams and their associations.

nations of yang and yin within this three-line format, a set of eight basic trigrams, the bagua, is derived.

In feng shui, each of the bagua is assigned to one of the Eight Entrances (or eight cardinal points of the compass). Each trigram represents a different natural force or phenomenon, and each of these is linked in turn to one of the Five Elements. Moreover, each of the Eight Trigrams represents a beneficiary for one of the Eight Entrances; that is, the type of person (in terms of age and gender) who will derive special benefit from a particular entrance. For example, the south entrance, whose trigram is Li, is beneficial for a young lady or the adult daughter of a household. Figure 14 is a comprehensive table of the relationships between the entrances and trigrams, the beneficiaries, the forces of nature, and the Five Elements.

12
A pause for reflection

LET'S TAKE A BREAK HERE. So far we have learned quite a lot about feng shui. We have seen how to locate the qi center of a space, and how to use the the Nine Stars, Eight Entrances, and the bagua for spatial analysis and the determination of good and bad sectors and directions. We have also touched on a number of other factors that influence the feng shui of a given site.

Readers should not be dismayed by the complex interplay of all these symbols and associations. The folk art of feng shui draws information from a wide range of sources and a rich tradition of ancient cosmological thought, and for this reason it can be daunting for the beginning practitioner. All of this feng shui lore is useful, but readers do not have to memorize it or even understand all of it at this point. Think of it instead as a kit of tools for analyzing and transforming your environment. You do not have to use every tool at once. But the more you work with them, the more they will fit your hands and accommodate your sensibility, and eventually they will help you generate creative images, concepts, motifs, and designs for remaking your living and working environment in ways that will nourish a positive attitude and a positive way of life.

This is why we have based this book on the traditional Nine Stars, Eight Entrances, and Bagua Combination method. Despite its complexity, it gives us a solid set of procedures based upon history and tradition. This ancient method is a gem in the Chinese folk art of feng shui. It has a logic and a substance all its own; as with a bottle of aged wine, or a lasting friendship, it has stood the test of time and should be savored accordingly. Many current practitioners of feng shui avoid such traditional schools, taking shortcuts and using simplified methods instead. This is fine, valid, and quite practical; we are all for it! But neglecting the traditional schools may also mean missing something interesting and valuable, to say nothing of the loss to the world's cultural heritage if such ancient art forms were completely abandoned.

Besides, the Nine Stars Method is not that difficult once explained. We have covered its most important elements and you have already learned how to do the basics of feng shui analysis using its ancient techniques. A thousand congratulations to all! In the second half of this book, we will gain greater familiarity with the method, apply what we have learned, and explore a number of helpful hints and tips for using feng shui to improve the quality of our environment and our lives.

PART TWO

Applied Feng Shui

A SAMPLE SPATIAL ANALYSIS

In Part One of this book we learned something of the history and theory of feng shui and the fundamentals of spatial analysis using the Nine Stars method. In this section, we will apply this method to the analysis of a simple structure. An old Chinese proverb says that "a little sparrow has all the characteristics of larger birds." This is true of spatial arrangements as well. The techniques we are learning can be applied to the most complex structures and architectural plans, but it is better to use a simple structure as a point of departure so that there will be no confusion regarding the fundamental principles.

As an example, let's consider the space shown in Figure 15, an ordinary small bedroom with three windows, a main entrance, and a side entrance secured by a pair of locking sliding doors that open onto an outside patio (which could also represent the backyard of a small house).

As we learned earlier, the qi center is the first thing we must locate. This is easy, for the room we are considering is a very simple geometric form. Once we have established the qi center, we postion ourselves there, and using a small conventional compass, we record the eight cardinal directions from this orientation point.

Once the eight directions are noted, we see that the main entrance to this room faces south. Now return to chart of the Eight Entrances in Figure 12. Find the row for the south entrance, and reading across you will find the directions and their associated stars: the east is ruled by Life and Growth, southeast by Heavenly Healing, northeast by Disaster, southwest by Six Conflicts, west by the Five Ghosts, north by Continuity, and northwest by Death. The eighth compass point is occupied by the entrance itself, to the south.

Having completed this basic orientation, we can now begin to see where the good and bad (or positive and negative) sectors are in this room. In the simplest terms we have four good sectors (the southern entrance, north, east, and southeast), three bad sectors (northeast, northwest, and southwest), and one tricky sector (the west). All of this information can then be mapped onto the space as shown in Figure 15. Now we can begin the main part of our analysis, taking the space sector by sector, starting with the main entrance.

South   Because it is occupied by the main entrance, the south sector does not have an associated star. Instead, it is associated with one of the bagua, or Eight Trigrams, as shown in the chart given in Figure 14. There we see that the trigram for a south entrance is Li, and that this is a very good direction indeed. As we learned earlier, the south is the domain of the Red Bird, which represents the southern sun. Its element is fire, a symbol of energy and vitality that may extend its influence to the attitudes and temperament of the person living in

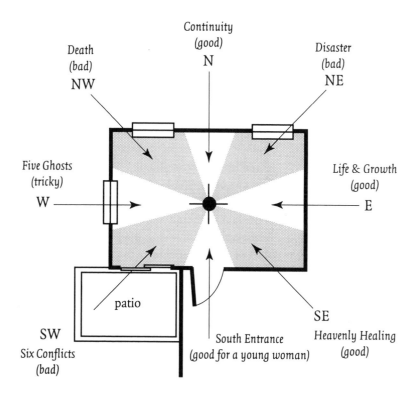

Continuity
(good)
N

Death
(bad)
NW

Disaster
(bad)
NE

Five Ghosts
(tricky)
W

Life & Growth
(good)
E

patio

SE
Heavenly Healing
(good)

SW
Six Conflicts
(bad)

South Entrance
(good for a young woman)

FIGURE 15.

A sample room for analysis.

this space. And if we look at the column in Figure 14 for the beneficiaries of each entrance, we find that a dwelling with a southern main entrance is especially beneficial for a young woman or an adult daughter of a family. This does not mean that such a space is not good for people of other ages or the opposite sex. But a young woman will derive special and positive value from inhabiting a space such as this.

In any case, the Li entrance is a very positive and useful one, especially if, as in this case, its opposite sector (north) is also a good one. As we shall see throughout this book, things in feng shui are all interrelated, and knowing the right balance and proportions of them is the basis of this art. It is a lot like cooking a successful meal or conducting an orchestra. Good positioning of a dwelling can be enhanced in various ways, and bad locations can be modified or ameliorated. But the direction of the main entrance of a building, as well as the overall orientation of the building on its site, are of crucial importance—like the main ingredient in a recipe or the keynote of a piece of music. To the ancient Chinese, such issues were not to be decided without considerable and serious thought as to the possible influence on the prosperity and well-being of the people who might be living and working there for generations to come. So whoever sited the main entrance to our hypothetical bedroom did their work well, from the point of view of feng shui. Now let's turn to the other favorable sectors, and see how they influence this space.

North   In this case, north is a positive sector, ruled by the star Continuity. Structurally, it is occupied by the north wall of the bedroom, with a window just off either of its two ends. As we saw earlier, a north wall with openings in it is dangerous, because it is exposed to the power of the Dark Warrior of the North, Zhen Wu, and his minions the Turtle and the Snake.

In this room, however, the portion of the wall located within the north sector is solid and protective, though the two windows at either end of it fall into bad sectors. Moreover, the potential danger of the north is further offset by the fact that in this case it is ruled by a good star (Continuity) and is also located directly across from the very positive southern entrance.

This is a good demonstration of the way in which various factors interact in feng shui, showing how a potentially negative direction can be neutralized by the influence of a positive star and balanced by a good entrance. It should be noted, however, that the opposite can be true. A fundamentally good direction can, by accident of location, be positioned within a bad star sector, and then weakened even further by bad arrangement of furniture and other objects. Consider your own living and working spaces—are you the right person in the wrong setting? Check and see!

Here, the fact that north is ruled by Continuity means that this star's positive influence will help warm this usually chilly sector. A good sector also gives us greater freedom for creativity in arranging objects to enhance it. We might borrow some fire elements from the sunny south—such as radiators or baseboard heating—to install along this north wall and dispel the winter's chill. This is also a good sector in which to place furniture for daily use, such as a chair, a love seat, or a small desk. This would not, however, be an appropriate location for a bed, since this sector is directly opposite the entrance, and placing a bed facing an entrance is harmful (something we will discuss in greater detail later). Since there are two more good sectors in this room, there is no need to place an important piece of furniture like a bed along the north wall of the room.

Wall-mounted light fixtures, paintings, or other decorative touches would be welcome here; but a simple, good clean wall is also splendid. We will explore the many uses of color in feng shui in a separate section, but here a white or warm beige would be most appropriate.

East and Southeast These are the two remaining positive sectors in this room, ruled respectively by the stars Life and Growth and Heavenly Healing. Because of this, they are safe, and permit a great deal of freedom in arranging furniture and other elements. We have plenty of options here, including placing a bed on the quiet *yin* side of the room, away from the active *yang* energy of windows and doors, insuring peace and privacy. Like the good north sector we have just visited, these two sectors encourage readers to freely position items such as a bed, chairs, a dresser, corner table, lamps and light fixtures, houseplants, and so on. Use your visual sense to achieve a harmonious balance of these objects, adding a colorful highlight here and there for punctuation.

For readers who want to experiment with color, suggested colors would be light blue for the east sector and light green for the southeast. Color can be drawn from many sources besides paint and wallpapers, curtains, and the like. Remember that you have nature's own palette available in the form of plants and flowers. The most important thing, of course, is a sense of overall color harmony. Read the section on color in feng shui later in this book to learn more of the legends and symbolic significance of color, which was very important in ancient China for ritual and ceremonial purposes.

Northeast We now come to the troublesome, negative sectors of the room. But these sectors are also perhaps the most interesting, presenting many challenging opportunities to exercise and express your skill in placing objects. As all dancers know, the most beautiful and creative steps on stage are the dangerous ones! Readers should learn from this and not avoid the bad sectors, where great acts of balance can be achieved. The trick is to neutralize and compensate for these bad sectors by knowing what to do, and you will soon know plenty about that. The first of the bad sectors is the northeast, ruled here by Disaster. The window located here compounds the problem. It will let in drafts on cold windy nights, but left unmodified it will also be a source of harsh, unregulated sunlight. This is bad for plants, colored materials, and furniture, and, according to feng shui, it is also bad for people.

Do not place a bed, desk, or sofa here; this should not be a sector in which people should gather or spend extended periods of time. It is a good place to put bookcases, or a television, VCR, or sound system. A standing lamp or upward-reflecting floor lamp will help ease this sector, as will a wall decoration in warm colors. Plants could also be useful; either a large, thorny cactus plant to confront the Disaster sector, or the more gentle approach of a small basin of water with greenery and flowers to soften this troublesome area. As always, use your imagination and follow an approach that fits your personality.

This sector may also require the placement of special good luck objects such as antique Chinese coins or a red Daoist talisman like the ones included in this book. If you prefer, this would also be a good place for a religious statuette or painting.

This is the Death sector, although once we have located it, it shouldn't worry us too deeply, since we have many techniques for dealing with it. But the Death sector is the most challenging of all the bad sectors in feng shui, and if it is not located and neutralized, it is potentially the most harmful.

Northwest

In our example, there is also a window here; not a desirable thing to have in a bad sector like this. A radiator or baseboard heating element will warm up this spot somewhat. Thick curtains and blinds are a good idea, and warm colors will also give life to this area on chilly nights, as will a floor lamp or other upward-reflecting light. A large container or vase of water with greenery will also do the job of stabilizing this area. Placing an audio system or a television here to create sound and movement to stimulate this space is another possibility. But whatever else you do, it is recommended that somewhere in this sector you keep a good luck charm on permanent display, something strong and sacred. What this might be depends on you; it might be a string of antique Chinese coins tied with a red silk cord, a Daoist talisman, an old Bible or prayer book, a string of prayer beads, a Seven Stars sword, a statue of a tiger, lion, or dragon, a Buddha, an angel, or some other religious image. Feng shui professionals know the Death sector can be the most interesting spot to do creative things, because this is where unfavorable influences can be challenged and overcome.

Southwest   The southwest sector in this room, governed by Six Conflicts, is not a good sector, but at the same time, not a deadly one. The problem we have here is the set of sliding glass doors, which leave the room open and vulnerable to greater danger and potential conflict, mostly coming into the room from outside. Such a door must be well-guarded and secured at all times.

Since this large pair of sliding glass doors is transparent and not structural, in feng shui it is regarded as an opening like a large window. Sunlight from this southwest sector is not as friendly as from the south, and it is not desirable to have one's room unprotected from the pouring in of harsh afternoon sunlight. This is too large a dose of *yang* energy, to say nothing of the lack of privacy, and the noise from outside that these doors could admit. This opening requires regulation and carefully placed objects to ward off bad spirits. But we are lucky that this open corner wall section is not in the Death sector, for if it were, the glass doors would have to be relocated to another sector and the opening walled in. As it is, the situation is manageable.

We will need heavy curtains and vertical blinds to shut out unwanted glare, noise, and other conflicts. The curtains should always be at least three-quarters drawn to keep out bad influences and restore harmony to the room. In winter you will want to make sure this entrance is well sealed, the curtains drawn, and perhaps even a baseboard heater added. An awning extending out over the patio and exterior storm doors may also help. A Daoist paper talisman selected from among those included in the book is also recommended. It can be posted on the interior wall beside the sliding doors. Even on summer nights, blinds and curtains are useful to prevent a chill coming from the southwest corner. In summer, arrange a series of green plants as a visual screen to deflect unfavorable influences from entering the room.

The west sector of this room is the Five Ghosts sector; not a bad one, but tricky if not attended to properly. It is an interesting sector to work with. In our example, this Five Ghosts sector has a window,   *West* which may open to both good and bad opportunities and forces. Therefore it must be guarded for its unpredictability. Be friendly to this sector, and try to nourish a good relationship with it. One way to do this is with water, since the natural association for the westerly direction is wetlands (water and earth). Water nourishes all the good things in life, from wealth and fame to romance. The west is also the domain of the White Tiger, whose element is metal. In the Five Elements theory we discussed earlier, water, earth, and metal all complement one another. Feng shui professionals love the west wall of a space, and often use it as the spot to achieve the maximum good for their clients.

There are many objects from which the reader can select to pacify and please this tricky Five Ghosts sector when it is located in the west: an aquarium with fish, green plants and flowers,or any other interior design item containing water elements, including a painting or other image of water, such as a seascape. However, in our example, the wall has a window in it, and we need to use blinds or curtains to protect water or objects containing water from overexposure to the hostile afternoon sun. Other possible enhancements are a good luck charm, a talisman, a string of antique coins, or a small and friendly image of the Buddha or an angel. But, as always, there is no need to overdo it and clutter things up. Use your judgment and taste. Even a simple large vase with water and greenery might do the job. A clock, a floor lamp, or a comfortable rocking chair might also provide activity and movement to vitalize this sector. Good ideas do not have to be expensive!

This completes our sample spatial analysis. By now the reader should have a good grasp of the fundamentals of feng shui analysis using the Nine Stars method. We have seen how to locate all the good and bad sectors, as well as a number of practical suggestions for how to enhance the good elements and neutralize the bad ones in a specific setting. The sections of the book following this one are a compendium of further suggestions of this kind, grouped into major categories for ease of use. These ideas and recommendations are generally shared and recognized by many other schools of feng shui in addition to the one we have followed in this book.

ENVIRONMENTAL FACTORS

Water Water is a very useful tool in feng shui. The earliest text dealing with this subject was written by the legendary Guo Pu (276–324 AD) whose discourses were later collected, edited, and revised during the Tang and Song dynasties. He wrote that qi and the human soul were united when a person was alive, but disintegrated upon death. According to Guo, "When qi is exposed to wind, it will be hurt or scattered. Upon the presence of water, it stays." This means that a person's qi depends on the nourishment of water, and protection from disturbance by wind. Wherever there is water, there will be life and future prosperity.

Guo is also well known for his writings on Five Elements theory and for his innovative four-part classification of geographical forms. He is the source of the popular feng shui teaching that "mountains surround and water embraces," referring to the use of water to embrace and nourish positive forces and the use of mountains as barriers to protect qi from being disrupted and scattered by wind. Thus, from very early in the historical development of feng shui theory, water and objects related to it have been regarded as essential to nourish and protect growth and good fortune and to counter or resolve negative influences.

In contemporary feng shui, water represents wealth. It has the magical power of dissolving unfriendly elements, both indoors and out. Water and objects containing it (fish tanks, fountains, vases of live flowers and greens, a basin or large bowl with water) will be welcome additions to the decor of living rooms, bedrooms, studies, work areas, and entryways. The ideal location for these elements is in the west sector of a space or along the west wall. If this is not possible, northwest or southeast corners are also good for arrangements involving water.

The qi center of a space should be kept free and airy, but water is always welcome there. Do not block the qi center with a solid, heavy piece of furniture. If you want any type of furnishing at the qi center, let it be a low coffee table, airy and open underneath, with a vase of water and flowers (not cactuses) on top. For commercial spaces, an auspicious arrangement would be a large restaurant kitchen or bar with the sinks located along the west wall or in a favorable sector according to the Nine Stars analysis. For larger public or outdoor projects, a fountain or a garden with a small pond is excellent as the focal point of the space.

The symbolic meaning of numbers is of crucial importance in feng shui, and there is an ancient tradition of numerology and number magic in China. Myth and legend trace the origins of this tradition back to Emperor Yu of the Xia dynasty, who is supposed to have lived about 2000 BC. One of Emperor Yu's famous exploits was the inauguration of huge flood-control projects to protect China's people and agriculture from the ravages of the unruly Yellow River. One day, while Emperor Yu was engaged in this work, a great sea turtle with the head of a dragon emerged from the river. On its shell and body was a pattern of colored dots forming the square of magic numbers known as the Luo Shu (see Figure 16). Within the Luo Shu magic square are nine smaller squares known as the Nine Palaces, each occupied by a number. One can read the numbers in any direction—left, right, up, down, or diagonally—and the sum will be fifteen. Fifteen is a compound of five and ten, five representing honor and ten representing unity and completion. The Chinese character for ten is written like a cross with four equal arms, in turn symbolizing the four directions existing in harmony and balance. Figure 17 shows the Luo Shu numbers in a more elaborate arrangement that gives their relationship to the eight cardinal directions, the Five Elements, and the Eight Trigrams of the Yijing. (Note that in Figures 17–19, south appears at the top, in accordance with Chinese custom).

The number ten is not included in the Luo Shu magic square, because it is an unspoken symbol representing sacredness, worship, and homage to all the gods. The numbers from one to nine are the basic ordinal numbers while ten is the final unifier.

FIGURE 16.

The Luo Shu magic
number square.

4	9	2
3	5	7
8	1	6

The Chinese term for worship is *heshi*, meaning "harmony-ten," and is symbolized by placing the two hands together with palms and fingers joined, indicating the unity of all dualities and the wholeness of the mind in respect and homage. All of the Luo Shu numbers have complex associations in fortune-telling and divination, some of which are listed here.

One is the number of the gods and of the emperor, known as the Son of Heaven. One represents the peak, the pinnacle, the ultimate—the one and only! We mortals cannot occupy this number position for long, for it can be lonely and dangerous. We are not divine, and only divinity can hold this position permanently.

Two, representing a pair or couple, is a happy number, and auspicious for events such as birthdays, weddings, and festivals. Two also represents the balance of the *yin* and *yang* forces that together form the *taiji*, or origin of all things. Two-line good luck poems called *dui* are inscribed on red paper and displayed on both sides of the main entrance of a dwelling or shop during the Chinese New Year.

Three is regarded as the most stable number, as a tripod is one of the most stable of all forms.

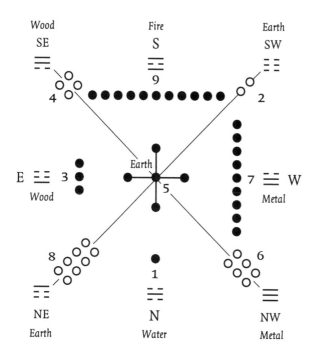

FIGURE 17.

The Luo Shu numbers displayed with the eight cardinal directions, the Five Elements, and the Eight Trigrams.

There is a Chinese phrase, *san san bu jin*, that means "three and three will never end," and expresses hope for longevity. Feng shui makes great use of numerology in arranging objects, and the number three is a particularly useful one to work with in enhancing the visual stability and unity of an environment.

Four is formed from two pairs, which should be auspicious, but in Chinese its pronunciation is identical to the word for "death," and because of this very unpleasant association, feng shui tries to avoid any arrangements involving the number four.

Five stands for honor, power, and authority. In ancient times, the imperial symbol was a five-clawed golden dragon. The emperor's throne was referred to as "the honor of five and nine," with five signifying the Five Directions (north, south, east, west, and center) and the five sacred mountains of China, and nine representing longevity and the eternal. The number five is also associated with the house god (*dizhu*) ruling over the prosperity and well-being of each Chinese home and protecting it from bad ghosts and evil spirits. Five is an excellent number to use in feng shui arrangements.

Six is a double of three, and therefore auspicious. The Chinese phrase *liu liu wu qiong* means "six and six will never go broke." This is because the the Chinese word for six, *liu*, has the same sound as the word for affluence. Three plus six is nine, and together these make up a trinity of lucky numbers. An arrangement employing any of them is good for neutralizing a bad directional sector or troublesome area.

Seven is a very powerful magic number, with deep mythological roots. There are seven visible stars in the Big Dipper, and a ceremonial Seven Stars sword is used in Daoist rituals, representing the power to dispel evil. The seventh night of the seventh lunar month is the time of a much-loved traditional Chinese festival celebrating the romance of a heavenly weaving girl and herd boy who are united once a year on this night by crossing the bridge formed by the Milky Way. In fairy tales and Daoist fables, a sequence of forty-nine days (seven times seven) is sacred, and associated with the gods; forty-nine days is also the prescribed period of mourning and remembrance after a person's death, after which the survivors should put aside their grief and resume their daily life. In feng shui, an arrangement of seven objects confers magic power and a sense of the sacred.

Eight is also a number with various religious associations. There are Eight Immortals in Daoist mythology, and Eight Treasures in the Buddhist tradition. There are also eight basic trigrams in the Yijing, and eight cardinal points on the compass. An octagonal table—called an Eight Immortals' table in China—symbolizes harmony and happiness. A coffee table or end table in this shape can be a good element to place in a bad sector. An octagonal window or an eight-sided vase are also good, and a bagua plaque (a octagonal wooden plaque carved and painted with the eight trigrams) is often hung over an entryway to overcome bad influences before they can enter a house.

And finally, nine is a very happy number. Its cousins are three and six, both auspicious. The Chinese word for nine (jiu) is a homophone with the word for longevity, and thus the number itself is associated with long life and good fortune.

The application of numerology to feng shui is flexible and should challenge your creativity and imagination. Numbers apply to almost any arrangement of furniture, objects, or features within a space. As we have seen, most of the nine basic numbers have positive associations, and you can make use of them in arrangements to enhance good sectors or help neutralize bad ones. You should, however, definitely try to avoid the use of the number four if possible, because of its association with death. Do not, for example, set a series of four objects, such as chairs, in a straight line. Chinese restaurants often use two small tables for two, separated by a very narrow space, to seat four people, and this "disconnected four" is a clever technique for dealing with this problem that can be applied in other situations as well. A series of four windows along one wall is a bad arrangement in feng shui; three or five would be better. Windows on different walls within a space adding up to a total of four may also be troublesome, but less harmful than four along a single wall. If you are stuck with such a group of windows in an existing space, the best remedy is to use thick curtains or a tall screen to close one of them permanently and block it from view.

Color The use of color in feng shui is quite ancient, deriving from Daoist mystical practices. From early times color has been used by Daoist priests and shamans to ward off evil spirits, pray for rain, communicate with the gods when asking advice on important matters, to heal sickness, and to avert misfortune. It has a strong association with numerology, going back to the Luo Shu of Emperor Yu described in the preceding section. The magic numbers Emperor Yu found on the sea turtle appeared as patterns of colored dots, and thus each of the nine basic numbers and nine directions (the eight cardinal directions plus the center) has a color connected with it. The associations between color, number, and direction were further codified by Emperor Wen of the Zhou dynasty (1100–771 BC), and his diagram of their relationships, known as the "After Heaven" diagram, is shown in Figure 18.

Color, number, and direction all figure importantly in Daoist ritual. On a Daoist altar, silk flags of the appropriate colors are hung to correspond to each of the directions. The altar is usually further decorated with talismans and other banners,

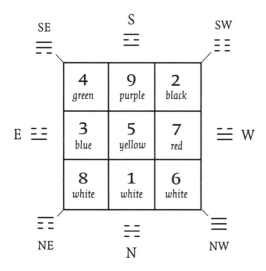

FIGURE 18.

The "After Heaven"
diagram of Emperor Wen

an incense burner, a water bowl, candles, and a Seven Stars sword of metal or wood symbolizing the authority of the Big Dipper and the North Star. Another important ritual implement is a fly whisk, usually made from horsehair or flax fibers, which is used to brush away evil spirits and to purify the room.

In ancient times, the Daoist priest would recite the names of the gods, chant prayers, and make prostrations before the altar, after which he would fall into a trance and perform a dance called the Yubu ("Steps of Emperor Yu"). The purpose of the dance was to importune the gods to manifest their magical powers and compassion for the benefit of mankind. The means of enlisting this power and bringing it down to earth was to link the various numbers of the Luo Shu magic square in prescribed patterns and arithmetical sequences through the steps of the dance itself. The colored

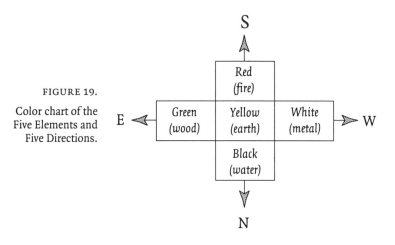

FIGURE 19.

Color chart of the
Five Elements and
Five Directions.

flags and banners keyed to the Luo Shu numbers
and the cardinal directions oriented the priest in
his dance and helped him make his connection
with the gods. So we see that colors have a deep
association with sacred power and magic.

In addition to the "After Heaven" diagram (Figure
18), there is another, keyed to the Five Elements
and Five Directions, that readers may wish to
explore as an alternative (Figure 19). In this chart,
colors are given only for the center and the directions of the quadrant. However, The in-between
colors can be derived as follows: for the northeast,
grayish green; southeast, lavender; southwest,
pink; and northwest, light gray. Extensive use of a
broad palette of color is a relatively modern
phenomenon, and some feng shui traditionalists
might raise objections to it. But for readers who
love color and want to apply it effectively and beau-
tifully to their living spaces, let us borrow ideas
from the heavenly gods! In fact, selection of subtle
pastels and other mixed colors, avoiding the harsh
intensity and glare of high chroma, is a reasonable

way to maintain visual harmony, and above all feng shui is an art of harmony and balance.

There are two kinds of light, natural and artificial. Natural sunlight is beneficial and much sought after by apartment-hunters in big cities like New York, but beware of getting too much of a good thing. Excessive sunlight and reflected glare are considered harmful in feng shui. Unregulated direct sunlight damages colors, furniture, fabrics, and people. It causes wooden furniture to crack, warp, and split, and fades paint and other colors. It also harms green plants and causes dryness in interiors. Reflected glare from windows, mirrors, pools, and other bodies of water can also penetrate a living space in harmful ways. Both direct sunlight and reflected glare should be regulated with the use of shutters, blinds, curtains, awnings, or screens. The key, as always, is to create a harmonious and balanced environment.

Artificial lighting includes candles and gas and oil lamps as well as electricity. Using electrical lights as a tool in feng shui to enhance good luck is a practical and modern approach. But excessive artificial lighting is inappropriate, and glare from outside artificial lights directed into a living space is also considered bad feng shui. For example, a large commercial neon sign facing into a person's window is considered hostile and unfriendly. Problems such as this one must be attended to and regulated like natural sunlight. Shutters, curtains, blinds, and feng shui talismans may be employed to ease the situation.

One contemporary use of outdoor lights in feng shui is to mount them so that they reflect upon a wall or the facade of your house to enhance good luck. Exterior lights in the backyard and sideyards can also be very useful. Be careful with this, however, for it can be undesirable for one's neighbors if such lighting is not well regulated or is in direct view of the neighbors' windows. Inside the house, correct and appropriate use of lights can be very rewarding, and is especially effective in softening the hard edges of interior walls and corners. Indirect lighting or floor lamps that project their light upwards are good tools.

As mentioned earlier, keeping a lamp lit at night along the north wall can help protect this vulnerable sector. Table or floor lamps with shades in happy, warm colors can be helpful in other bad areas such as the Death, Disaster, Five Ghosts, and Six Conflicts sectors—or they can be arranged to enhance even a good sector, if you so desire. Just remember that the basic goal is to achieve balance, harmony, and serenity, and let your own good judgment be your guide.

ARCHITECTURAL FEATURES

Main entrance and windows The entrance and windows of your home are affected by the surrounding environment. For example, a large hard-edged object such as the corner of an opposing building can be a very harmful influence if it is pointed directly at your front door or one of your windows. The closer it is, the more damaging it can be to the people living inside, and even at a good distance, it is still considered unfriendly in feng shui terms. A large smokestack, tree trunk, telephone pole, or electri-

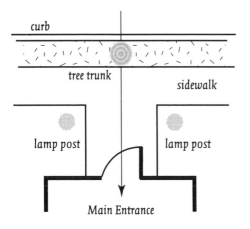

curb

tree trunk

sidewalk

lamp post

lamp post

Main Entrance

FIGURE 20.

Remedy for a tree trunk bisecting the centerline of a main entrance.

cal pole sited at the centerline of a window or entrance is also harmful. Correcting major, permanent threats such as these may be difficult, for a host of reasons. In some cases, the best solution may be to relocate to another house or apartment.

If this is not possible, there are various remedies that can be applied. In the case of a tree trunk or telephone pole bisecting the centerline of your main entrance, one such remedy is illustrated in *Figure 20*. As shown here, the owner of the house has installed two tall outdoor lamp posts on either side of the main entrance. This triangular arrangement (post-door-post) counterbalances the threat posed by the huge tree trunk. The two lamps serve as guards protecting the entrance, and at night their light will help ward off any intruders.

When hostile exterior objects such as building corners, smokestacks, and the like are visible from the entrance or windows but not lined up on their centers, the situation is less grave, but should still be attended to. One simple remedy to ease the situation is to hang a wooden *bagua* plaque over the entrance or window in question, either on the exterior or interior wall (the nature and function of the *bagua* plaque will be discussed in greater detail later). If hung outside, some people like to augment its beneficial influence by installing a small exterior light to shine on the plaque at night.

Neither the main entrance of a house nor the centerlines of windows should align with the large open entryway of a big building or with the entrance gate of a cemetery. The first is known as a "tiger's mouth," and is dangerous and unsettling; the inauspicious nature of the second situation needs little explanation. Remedies may be impossible, in which case it would be better to change residences. However, if the threatening elements are located at least several hundred feet away, it may be possible to ameliorate the situation by creative use of various screening devices to block the view (hanging plants, curtains, folding screens, and so forth).

The configuration of the front steps, main entrance, and foyer is a very important matter in the feng shui of a residence. These features should be given careful attention, not only in terms of the overall orientation of the house, but with regard to smaller details of their design. The exterior landing and the foyer must be reasonably level and generous in order to invite good fortune to come in and stay. It is particularly important to avoid an abrupt fall-off step only inches away from the threshold of the main entrance. This is not only a safety hazard, it is also a serious error in feng shui, for it will cause the Three Treasures of life, love, and prosperity to fall away. A simple remedy is to

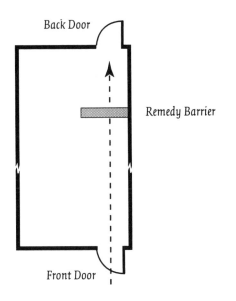

Back Door

Remedy Barrier

Front Door

FIGURE 21.

Remedy for front and back doors aligned on the same axis.

extend the exterior landing, making sure it is broad and generously proportioned, and that the steps are gradual and safe for everyone.

The orientation of doors relative to one another and to other architectural features is very important. The following are some common situations to watch out for.

A front door aligned on a straight and unobstructed axis with the back door of a residence is very undesirable. This situation allows qi to leak from the house, and is a harbinger of financial problems and other difficulties. If possible, relocate the back door or close it permanently. If this is not possible, there is another relatively simple solution, which is to set up a barrier or half-wall as shown in *Figure* 21 to interrupt through traffic from front to back. This will serve to retain qi and

Doors

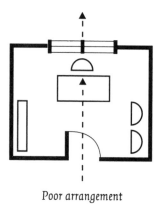 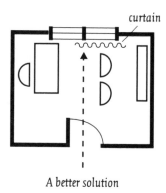

Poor arrangement   A better solution

FIGURE 22.

Door and window
alignments

other good influences, and benefit the people living in the space.

For the same reason, it is best to avoid having the door of a bedroom, office, or other room directly aligned with a window (Figure 22). If such a situation exists, do not compound the problem by placing a desk or bed on the same axis; this would be very unfavorable to the person using the space. Position the desk or bed in another, more protected part of the room, and use your imagination to invent creative solutions for masking or baffling the door-and-window alignment; a large hanging plant or partially drawn curtains screening the window are two possibilities.

The common placement of office doors directly facing each other along the same corridor or hallway in a fishbone pattern is another bad feng shui arrangement. This direct opposition of door against door will promote conflicts and poor spirit among colleagues and workers. It is better to offset the doors in a consecutive and orderly fashion. Obviously, this should be considered at the very beginning stages of office design.

Neither interior nor exterior doors in a residence should align directly with a staircase. Doors giving immediately unto stairs are a physical hazard to children and even adults, especially at night. Moreover, such an arrangement will bring conflict and financial instability to the occupants of the house. Nor should the entrance or doors to other rooms directly face the doorways of a toilet, kitchen, or bedroom. These are harmful feng shui situations, generating bad luck and conflict, and are bad for privacy as well! Unfortunately, remedies for such permanent architectural features as the location of doorways and entrances may be costly, and require the services of an architect or structural engineer.

The hard vertical edge of an inward-opening door (of the swinging, hinged type) is considered a "knife-edge" in feng shui (see Figure 23). By all means avoid positioning a desk, bed, easy chair, or sofa—any piece of furniture likely to be occupied by a person for any length of time—in such a way that this knife-edge swings or points toward it. This knife-edge promotes conflict and difficulty of all kinds, especially for the head of a household or a company. There are various remedies for this common danger. The simplest is to move your furniture away from the area so that it is not threatened. Another approach is to rehang the door so that it swings outward rather than inward, or to replace the swinging door with sliding door. But these are potentially expensive solutions. It may be cheaper and easier to solve the problem by hanging a good-sized vertical mirror on the opposite

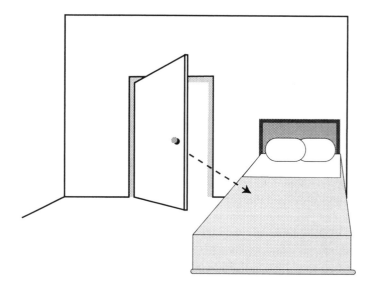

FIGURE 23.

The "knife-edge" of a door.

wall, reflecting the hard edge of the door and thus counterbalancing the threat of the knife-edge with its own mirror-image. And finally, those who are creative and enjoy handicrafts and sewing might design and construct a cloth jacket to cover the door's edge, smoothing its sharpness and hardness with rich folds and drapes of material ina a manner similar to a window curtain or a furniture covering. This can be both an inexpensive and fun way to solve this problem.

Interior corners and wall intersections

Ninety-degree angles and sharp intersections are not favored in feng shui. Rounded corners, curvilinear forms, and soft edges are preferred. The uncompromising sharp shapes and rectilinear forms of some interiors may be considered unfriendly. Modernist design in particular can sometimes produce intrusive and unsettling interior forms, full of odd angles and harsh intersections disturbing to the serenity of the home or office.

Again, rather than costly structural redesign, it is possible to arrive at inexpensive and creative solutions to achieve the feeling of harmony and organic form that is the hallmark of feng shui. Lighting may be the most effective technique to employ in smoothing the harsh edges of an interior. Strategic placement of floor lamps, indirect lighting, or a lamp set on a corner table can do much to soften hard edges and corners. Upward-reflecting lights can be installed behind sofas or vertical arrangements of potted plants. Skillful use of both light and color can work wonders in adding a sense of warmth, softness, and coziness to a space that might at first appear sharp and unfriendly.

Columns and ceiling beams are necessary archi- *Columns and beams* tectural features, essential to the structural integrity and safety of a home or other building. However, the location of columns and beams in relation to the interior space may be undesirable or unacceptable from the standpoint of feng shui, and this issue must be given attention.

For example, a large column centerlined on the main entrance or dominating the center of a room is a serious problem. In feng shui this is called a "heart-blocking pillar," and regarded as hostile and unfavorable to the people living or working in the space (Figure 24). A heart-blocking pillar will enhance conflicts and other problems, and the visual obstacle it presents will disturb people's minds as they encounter it on a daily basis. A remedy for this situation can be costly, because it is no simple matter to relocate either the column or the

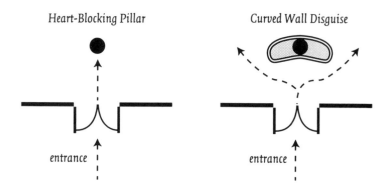

Heart-Blocking Pillar

Curved Wall Disguise

entrance

entrance

FIGURE 24.

A "heart-blocking pillar" and a possible remedy for it.

entrance. One solution is to discontinue the use of this entrance as the the main entrance, renovating or redecorating a side entrance to replace this troublesome one. If this is not possible, another remedy is to mask this heart-blocking pillar inside the friendlier shape of a curved partition wall encasing the pillar from floor to ceiling, as shown in Figure 24. Place a large green plant, a small artificial fountain, or a small tank with water plants at the foot of the wall inside which the column is buried. This curved partition wall and the water arrangement will do much to alleviate the bad feng shui of the heart-blocking pillar.

A large overhead beam can be another major difficulty. It is like the sword of Damocles, hanging over the heads of the people sitting or sleeping beneath it, threatening misfortune and even death (Figure 25). Unfortunately, beams are usually permanent structural features that cannot be easily removed or relocated. One remedy is a dropped or hung ceiling to disguise the beam. But in many cases this will not be sufficient to undo its baleful influence, and a sense of unease at the invisible

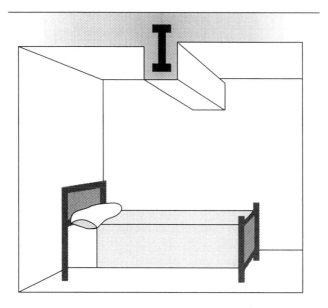

FIGURE 25.

A bed threatened by an
overhead beam.

danger lurking above will continue to unsettle the
occupants of the room. You should arrange your
furniture so that no pieces that will be occupied
by people (beds, desks, sofas, etc.) are located
directly beneath even a disguised beam. Because
hung ceilings often conceal them, it may be necessary to do a little detective work with structural
drawings or architectural blueprints to check out
where these big structural beams are located. You
need not worry about rafters, which are smaller
and pose no threat; nor do air ducts or plenums
present a problem, since they are hollow.

The location of the kitchen and bathrooms is
important because they directly affect the health
and well-being of the people living in the house. A
kitchen is the place where the stove, with its heat

*Location of kitchens
and bathrooms*

and fire, is located, and where all the sharp and pointed utensils are kept. Therefore, the kitchen is a locus of action, movement, heat, and *yang* energy. Never place a kitchen in the very center of a house or building, even though such a location may considered efficient by some designers. This is called a "burning heart" arrangement, and absolutely must be avoided. Daily cutting, chopping, frying, and roasting activities must not be situated at the *qi* center of the house, which should be left airy and unburdened! The kitchen must be located somewhere else, to the side, or at least off-center. Ancient Chinese would not even think of allowing a "burning-heart" kitchen location in their homes, and it makes sense to follow their example, since even modern stoves and ovens with vents and exhaust fans cannot get rid of all the smell, smoke, and grease of cooking, or the potential risk of fire.

Bathrooms and toilets are water-related features, and water is normally good in feng shui, but the association with wastes and the issue of privacy also affect the placement of these rooms within a house. Some feng shui practitioners actually prefer to place bathrooms and toilets in bad sectors (according to the Nine Stars directional analysis), for they believe that this will result in bad luck and bad influences being flushed or purged from the dwelling.

Heating and air conditioning

Artificial heat, like the natural heat energy from the sun, is a *yang* force. Heating units like radiators and baseboard heaters warm up cold areas on chilly nights and in the winter months. It is generally good to place these modern fixtures under windows along the cold northern wall, or in the northwest and northeast sectors from which cold winds may come. Air conditioners, because of the cold nature of their energy, may be considered *yin* forces. They are excellent devices to neutralize the hot *yang* force of summer, but if used excessively can cause chills and illness. Because they pull in air from outside, they are similar to open windows, which require attention and regulation. The column of chilled air thrown out by an air conditioner can be harmful to younger children and elderly people, and a decorative curtain or screen may be required to deflect its path from sitting or sleeping areas.

FENG SHUI TOOLS

A number of objects are used as tools in feng shui to counter bad influences and enhance positive ones, or to provide special protection to the residents of a house. The following sections discuss some of the more popular of these tools and how they are used by feng shui practitioners.

Mirrors

Mirrors, in all their various shapes, sizes, and forms, are powerful tools in feng shui. They have the power to deflect as well as to reflect; to ward off evil and to enhance good. However, because mirrors possess these interesting characteristics and powers, they should not be used casually. Sometimes mirrors are initiated for feng shui use by priests or shamans, with prayers and rituals developed for this purpose . A mirror of this kind is not a toy, nor a decorative object to have fun with, or freely move around. It is a serious device, meant to be positioned at a specific point to influence the feng shui of a house in a specific way.

In fact, there is a very special type of mirror that the reader will not have occasion to use, but is interesting to know about nonetheless. This is an exorcist's mirror, used by a trained priest or shaman to capture an evil spirit or to absorb malevolent forces, after which it is shattered and the shards thrown into the deep sea or buried underground. Used only when there has been a serious illness or tragedy, these magic mirrors are dangerous tools. Even shamans are very careful in handling them, because of the bad karma that can adhere to them.

In general, however, mirrors (especially ordinary ones) are good tools with many positive and beneficial uses, such as the following:

A series of wall mirrors can be used to reflect and enhance both natural and artificial light in dark spaces that have an excess of yin energy. Decorative wall mirrors of this sort have the added value of creating an illusion of greater depth and spaciousness in cramped or narrow rooms.

Mirrors can be mounted on the north wall of a room to reflect natural light coming from the sunny south; they can also be used in dark corners or dead-end corridors to brighten up dark areas and relieve the gloom.

As noted earlier, a good-sized mirror can also be used to counter the "knife-edge" of an inward-opening door. If used in a bedroom, readers should take care that the mirror does not reflect the head of the bed, or, ideally, any other part of it (see

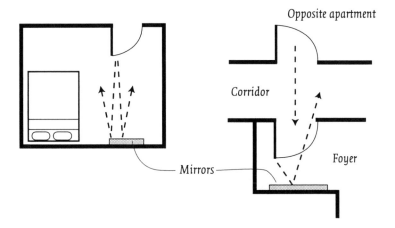

FIGURE 26.

Figure 26). The mirror should be offset or screened with pleasant curtains to avoid this. Nor should a mirror reflect the head and body of a person seated at a desk or table; it is not good for a person to be encountering his or her own image repeatedly while seated in one place for any length of time.

Mirrors can also be put to excellent use in foyers or entryways (*Figure 26*). A well-proportioned wall mirror hung in a dark foyer can add some life to that space and make it quite pleasant; it will also reflect the "knife-edge" of the door, and most doors of this kind open inward. A mirror is also a very good precaution if the entrance to your apartment is directly opposite that of a neighbor—something that occurs quite frequently, but is regarded as bad feng shui, likely to promote conflict and hostility. A mirror in the entryway can help alleviate this situation, deflecting bad influences before they can harm other areas of the home.

Use of mirrors in a bedroom and foyer.

87

Geometric shapes and forms

Geometric shapes and forms are more commonly encountered in discussions of outdoor feng shui, in which they are used to analyze and characterize various aspects of the terrain and landscape. But the geometry of interiors is significant as well. As noted earlier, Daoist cosmological thought classifies all things according to the Five Elements (metal, water, wood, fire, and earth) and their combinations, which can be conflicting or complementary. Figure 27 shows the application of Five Elements theory to basic geometric forms. These associations can be used in interior feng shui to neutralize or compensate for a bad sector. For example, if the entrance to a house is located on the east, that puts the west sector in the domain of Death. But west is also associated with water, and this positive association can be enhanced by placing a curvilinear piece of furniture—a water form—in this area. Creative readers should have fun considering the design possibilities inspired by the use of geometric forms as embodiments of the Five Elements, and applying them to harmonize their living space. Even structural elements like windows can be modified in shape to influence the feng shui of a room.

Paintings and sculpture

Works of art can be used very effectively in feng shui. One popular technique is to hang a painting with warm colors and lush scenery to add life to a cold northern wall. A painting of a lake or other calm body of water is welcome on a west wall, which is the domain of the White Tiger and is associated with water and wetlands. And paintings with religious motifs or symbols are good to display in a bad directional sector to offset its influence.

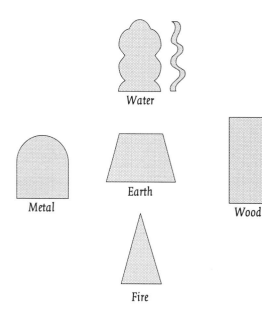

Water

Metal

Earth

Wood

Fire

FIGURE 27.

Geometric forms associated with the Five Elements.

Sculptures such as a pair of *fu* dogs, lions, or tigers make good guardians for the entrances of houses or other buildings. Smaller versions of them can be placed in unfriendly sectors inside a house or room to ward off bad influences. Also good for this purpose are wooden dragon masks, or religious figures such as angels or a statue of Guanyin, Goddess of Mercy. A religious text—a Bible, Koran, or collection of Buddhist sutras—can also be placed in a bad sector to improve it.

Coins

Old coins have long been regarded as good luck charms, not only by the Chinese, but by many cultures. In the West, antique coins are often mounted in rings and other jewelry for luck as well as style. But the Chinese folk tradition has some special customs involving coins.

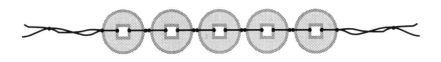

FIGURE 28.

A lucky string of five antique Chinese coins.

One is the small red paper envelopes for wrapping New Year's "good luck" money. These are sold in many Chinese stores, or readers can make their own by folding a square of red paper around a pair of coins, securing them neatly inside. Make four such envelopes—the coins can be Chinese or Western, old or new—and attach each one to the four corners of your bed or to the four legs of a desk or worktable. Position the envelopes discreetly, so they are not directly exposed to the view of others. Similar envelopes may be placed, if you wish, at the four main corners of your house or apartment, or atop the frame or molding of a doorway, where a single envelope is tidy and sufficient to enhance good fortune.

Antique Chinese coins, the kind with square holes in their centers, are also frequently joined in strings of three, five, or seven. Two red cords, preferably of silk, are used to link them, for red is the color of happiness. The cords are passed through the holes in the coins and knotted as shown in *Figure 28*. Strings of coins such as this one are hung over the main entrance to a dwelling for good luck and protection from evil influences. They are also useful tools in neutralizing bad directional sectors such as Disaster and Death. They can be hung horizontally between two nails (a good way to place them over a doorway), or vertically from a single one (when space is restricted).

Modern coins can also be used to counterbalance a bad sector. On a small table or wall shelf, set out five cups with lids. Fill each cup with water, place a penny, nickel, or dime in it, and cover the cup with the lid to slow evaporation. Change the water when needed. If this seems overly complicated, an arrangement of five little talismanic animals—tigers, bears, dragons, lions, or a combination thereof—can be used to similar effect.

Jade

Ancient Chinese considered jade (nephrite or jadite) and objects carved from it to be good luck charms. They believed jade to be a sacred stone given as a gift from heaven to people on earth. In the old days, travelers always tied a jade disk or a jade pendant to their belt for safety and good fortune on their journeys, and jade is still favored by many Asians in jewelry for both men and women. In a manner similar to antique coins, small jade pieces or figurines can be used to tone down unfavorable sectors.

Trees and plants

Trees or shrubs can be used as a visual screen to soften an unpleasant view in front of a main entrance or across the street. For entrances and windows facing a cemetery, or threatened by some other object across the street, plant a stand of small Guanyin bamboo (which does not grow taller than eight or nine feet) to screen the view. Smaller pine trees, or a fence of thorny red roses will also work. Consult an expert on trees and shrubs to find out what kind might be most appropriate for your residence in terms of height, growth pattern, care and maintenance, and cost.

For less threatening views, such as an unpleasant building in the distance, a smokestack, or a

FIGURE 29.
A *bagua* plaque.

large vacant lot, a smaller arrangement of five potted cactus plants along an interior window ledge
can also serve as a visual screen and deflector of
bad influences. In addition, if a person prefers a
confrontational approach to countering a bad sector inside a house, a large cactus plant may work.
However, a cactus should absolutely not be placed
at the qi center of a space or along the west wall;
these areas can be harmed by thorns and dryness.
Moreover, for the worst sectors, such as Death and
Disaster, it is sometimes unadvisable to be too
confrontational—using good luck talismans or
objects to deflect or neutralize the bad influences
of these sectors may be a better idea.

A *bagua* plaque   A *bagua* plaque is usually octagonal, made of
wood, and emblazoned with the *bagua* (eight trigrams) and the *yin-yang* symbol (see Figure 29). It
is normally painted in red or yellow, plus other

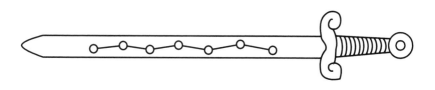

FIGURE 30.

A Seven Stars sword.

colors. Red is for happiness, and yellow symbolizes nobility, power, and stability. A golden yellow was the designated color for an emperor and his royal household in ancient China. Some versions may have a small round mirror in the center; others may have a yellow tiger head bearing the *bagua*. The *bagua* plaque is a very effective object for deflecting conflicts and bad influences, and it can be discreetly placed on a wall, shelf, or desktop at bad directional sectors inside a house. Many Chinese hang one outside over their main entrance to ward off unpleasant things coming to their front door. Some like to add a small reflected light shining at the sign at night for extra emphasis and effect.

Readers can buy a *bagua* plaque in a Chinese store. But it is always fun to make things, and you may want to try making your own *bagua* plaque, following the basic design provided here, and painting it in various colors. Then it will be truly yours, and have even more value as a protector of your home.

A Seven Stars sword

This is a ceremonial and decorative sword of either metal or wood, with seven circles representing each of the seven visible stars of the Big Dipper displayed on the middle of both sides of the blade (*Figure 30*). The stars are joined together by a thin zigzag line, as shown here, to symbolize the Big Dipper and its alliance with the North Star to

FIGURE 31.

A Chinese coin sword.

promote justice and counter evil. The stars are usually engraved or inlaid into the blade. But if readers want to make their own Seven Stars sword, the stars can be painted on, in either yellow or white. This decorative sword is intended to be hung horizontally over windows with unpleasant views or on the wall of bad sectors inside a house.

A variant on this type of feng shui sword is the traditional coin sword, made of many antique Chinese coins stacked and strung together with red silk cords as shown in Figure 31. These coin swords are also intended to be hung on a wall or over a window. They are collector's items, and because of the number of antique coins needed to make them, they can be quite expensive even when you are lucky enough to find one.

Bells and wind bells

Bells and wind bells have recently become quite popular in feng shui arrangements. People hang them to attract good luck. In certain respects, however, bells are like mirrors; one must be careful in using them.

According to Chinese beliefs, the ringing of a bell creates a sound path joining heaven and the netherworld, with its connecting point here on earth. Contained within the sound of the bell are both sacred and profane, good and evil. Small metal wind bells are traditionally hung under the tips of the curving eaves of Buddhist or Daoist temples, pagodas, or sutra halls. During the daytime the wind tosses these bells, ringing them to disperse evil spirits and wandering ghosts; but after sundown, the bells become temporary lodgings for these spirits and ghosts until daybreak. The compassion and generosity of the priests and monks provides these sad spirits and wandering ghosts with these tiny lodging places. But the night winds and breezes tossing the bells also serves to remind the spirits that they are but transient visitors.

Among modern feng shui practitioners, the use of bells to enhance good luck is a controversial practice. Some favor it because it is a new trend; but others think it unwise. Certainly older practitioners prefer bells and wind bells to be restricted to religious sites such as altars, temples, and monasteries, and to be used only for religious rituals, such as exorcisms or ceremonies for dispelling sickness. Moreover, if a bell is hung in an interior for a particular feng shui function, but not properly initiated by a Daoist priest or other adept, it may eventually become a comfortable home for bad spirits that will enter the house to reside there. These are points for anyone thinking of using bells to contemplate.

Hanging bells for decoration and celebrations is fun and joyful, and should not have adverse side effects. We are all for that. However, the use of a bell as a feng shui tool at a specific location is another matter, and requires care and good judgment. As with mirrors, having bells in a house is not a bad thing at all. But use bells selectively, in full awareness of their power and their symbolic significance.

Daoist talismans   A set of Daoist talismans, printed on red paper, has been provided on the following pages as a special feature of this book, and the author invites readers to tear them out and place them at strategic points in their homes or offices. The history and significance of these good luck charms is described below.

Good luck charms of this kind are very popular among the Chinese, for they are inexpensive, easy to use, and quite decorative as well. Usually they are written by Daoist priests who initiate them with various religious rituals. In fact, these talismans are regarded as sacred "working orders" from a particular god commanding evil spirits to stay away. Talismans are sometimes written in cinnabar ink on strips of yellow rice paper, but for common household use, especially during New Year's or other happy festivals, they are generally written in black ink on red paper. Red hints of the Red Bird of the South—the sun—and symbolizes happiness. Because of the auspiciousness of the color, words from the gods written in red ink or on red paper are thought to gain even more authority and power.

The tradition of using written talismans to dispel evil started quite early in China. The form of the characters used on talismans is a special decorative cursive script, a composite of several ancient styles of calligraphy and seal inscriptions. Daoist legend relates that the making of written talismans began with the famous master Zhang Ling (also known as Zhang Daoling), who was born in 34 AD, in Jiangsu province on the eastern coast of China. He was regarded as one of the important early patriarchs of Daoism. Like his illustrious ancestor Zhang Liang (230?–185 BC), whom we

I

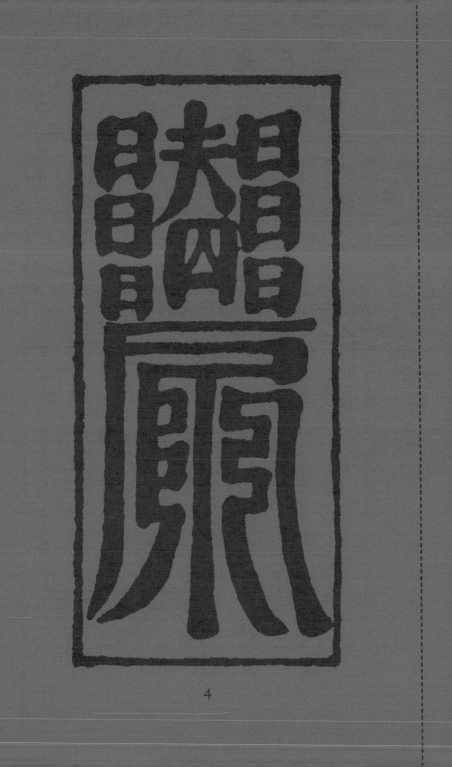

6

7

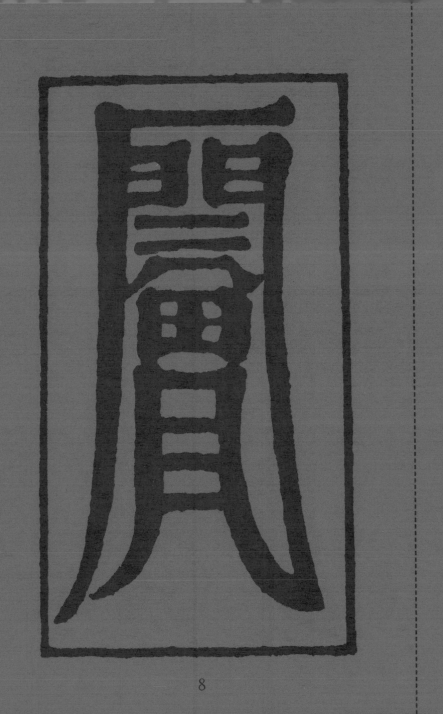

met in Part One of this book, Zhang Daoling was a great scholar of astrology and numerology. By middle age, he was known far and wide for his knowledge and ability, and was summoned by the emperor to serve at the imperial court. However, like his distant grandpa Zhang Liang, he did not heed this summons, and instead ventured deep into the mountains and forests to live as a recluse and commune with the gods. After many years of wandering throughout China, he settled in the deep wilderness of Mount Qingcheng in what is now Sichuan province. He was believed to have attained immortality and, as legend has it, lived to the age of 122 on this earth, which he "left" in the year 156 AD. Before he did, he received instructions from the heavenly gods to write down Daoist scripts and talismans that would aid and protect people and cure them of their ills.

Many centuries later, during the Southern Song dynasty (1127–1279 AD), another great-great-great grandson of the Zhang family by the name of Zhang Sanfeng also became a famous and revered master of the Daoist religion. To this day, historians still do not know when Zhang Sanfeng was born or the date of his passing. By one account, he was born in 1247 and lived more than 120 years, that is, from the late Song dynasty through the Yuan and into the early Ming! Historians think there actually might have been two or three persons from the Zhang family that used the same name—which would also help explain the many volumes of important Daoist books written under that name.

At any rate, legend credits Zhang Sanfeng with the invention of *taijiquan*, the meditative exercises still popular today both in China and in the West (where they are perhaps better known as Tai Chi). He is also said to have received special communications from the gods to help free people from illness and difficulties, and to have "died" several times, coming back again to continue his work on earth. His techniques for writing and using Daoist talismans are regarded, along with *taijiquan*, as his most enduring legacy. Some talismans may have been added by his followers, but the majority of them, it is believed, are faithful copies of Zhang's originals, preserved through the centuries in both handwritten and printed versions.

The author has provided a representative sample of these talismans for the the readers' use. The calligraphic tradition of the original pictograms is followed, but all talismans are in the author's own handwriting and brush style. The following is a list of the talismans and a description of their significance and use.

1) *Inverted fu.* Technically speaking, this is not a Daoist talisman, but an ordinary good luck charm. Though it has become especially popular in modern times, the inverted *fu* has its origins in old provincial Chinese folk practices. Often seen in Chinese restaurants, stores, and houses, this charm is a red square of paper with the Chinese character *fu*—meaning prosperity or good fortune—written upside down on it in gold or black ink. The Chinese words "inverted" and "arrival" have the same sound (*dao*), though they are written with different characters. Thus an "inverted" *fu* is a visual pun signifying the "arrival" of good luck and happiness at the place where it is posted— usually at the main entrance to a restaurant, store, residence, or living room. Make sure that it is

hung properly in order to bring you all the good things you want!

2) *The Yuhuasi ("Master Jade Flower") talisman.* Representing purity, peace, and harmony, it can be posted anywhere in a room, but is especially useful to help neutralize a bad sector.

3) *An order from the gods to expel bad luck and disaster.* It may be posted anywhere, especially in a bad sector.

4) *Main entrance talisman.* This should be posted on an interior wall beside or above the main entrance of a residence to defend it against bad influences.

5) *Door talisman.* This may be posted on or near any of the interior doors of a house or apartment for good luck. It is particularly good for bedroom doors.

6) *Kitchen talisman.* This one is for the safety and harmony of the kitchen and to avert bad influences. It is a very popular talisman and can be posted next to an altar for the kitchen god, a common feature in many Chinese kitchens.

7) *Talisman against ghosts and spirits.* This talisman is an order from the gods to dispel any ghosts or evil spirits from a room at night. This is a very popular one for children and young people's bedrooms, and for anyone who is afraid of the dark.

8) *Personal safety and good luck talisman.* This is a very popular talisman to carry with you when you travel or leave your house for any period of time. It is good for everyone, and especially for children.

A FINAL EXERCISE

In the course of a hundred pages, we have covered a lot of ground together. We have learned the essentials of feng shui, beginning with an appreciation of its history and theoretical foundations, going on to master the various components of a Nine Stars analysis of a space, and then exploring the practical application of a variety of tools, tips, tricks, and talismans employed by feng shui masters. In this final section, we will review what we have learned, using the home shown in Figure 32 as a model.

Marginal notes give page or illustration numbers for quick review.

This is a relatively simple two-bedroom house or apartment, with two baths, a kitchen, and a single large living and dining area. The main entrance and the main living room are the most important areas in this residence—and indeed, in any residence. In analyzing the feng shui of a space and determining how to work with it, these main areas of human activity and the circulation of qi are of prime importance. It is from the qi center of the main living area that we chart the eight directional sectors used in our Nine Stars analysis, and thus discover the good and bad areas for the entire dwelling.

Pages 26–28.

Once we have located the qi center (in this case, remember to take into account the curved area formed by the front bay windows when assessing the space), we position ourselves there and use a compass to determine the eight cardinal directions (N, S, E, W, NE, SE, NW, SW) that in turn will give us the eight sectors for our Nine Stars analysis. As we learned earlier, each sector occupies 45°, or 22.5° on either side of its directional axis.

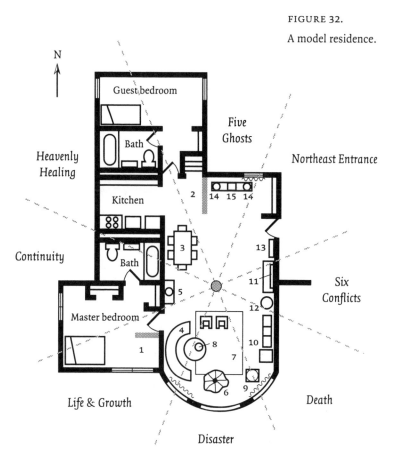

FIGURE 32.

A model residence.

N

Guest bedroom

Bath

Five
Ghosts

Heavenly
Healing

Northeast Entrance

Kitchen

2 14 15 14

3

13

Continuity

Bath

11

Six
Conflicts

5

12

Master bedroom

4

8

10

1

7

6   9

Life & Growth

Death

Disaster

1. Room divider
2. Masking wall
3. Dining table
4. Sofa
5. Goldfish bowl
6. Tree with talisman
7. Warm-colored carpet
8. Good luck charm

9. Large cactus
10. TV, stereo, VCR
11. Painting
12. Standing lamp
13. Display shelves
14. Lamps
15. Wooden bagua plaque

This compass reading tells us that the main entrance to this residence is in the northeast sector.

Figure 12, page 45.

We can then use the chart of the Eight Entrances to discover the other seven sectors for this particular space and their ruling stars. The results are already shown in *Figure 32*: reading clockwise from the northeast entrance, east is occupied by Six Conflicts, southeast by Death, south by Disaster, southwest by Life and Growth, west by Continuity, northwest by Heavenly Healing, and north by the Five Ghosts. This is a good time to review the sig-

Pages 36–40.

nificance of these sectors and their ruling stars, as this Nine Stars analysis forms the basis for everything else we will do with this space.

With the basic characteristics of this residence now established, let's test your understanding of feng shui based on the material we have covered. Try answering the following questions yourself; then read the answers, and if you want more information, refer to the pages of the book or the figures indicated in the marginal notes.

1) *The main entrance of this dwelling is to the northeast. Does this give special benefit to anyone?*

Yes. The northeast entrance is particularly aus- picious for a young boy or youngest son, including

Figure 14.

a young male head of a household. It will not be harmful to residents of other ages or of the oppo- site sex, but it will give a special boost to the for- tunes of any young man lucky enough to live here.

2) *Is the kitchen located in a good sector? How do you feel about its position relative to the main entrance?*

The kitchen is located in the Heavenly Healing sector, which is ideal, establishing a very positive association between health and nourishment. It is also set away from the center of the house, which is very important. But its position so close to the main entrance presents a tricky situation; they also come dangerously close to aligning on the same axis, which is even worse. However, a simple but effective remedy has been applied here: a masking wall that screens the kitchen from direct view of the entryway.

Pages 77–79

3) Rate the location of the master bedroom. Can you explain the positioning of the elements within it?

The master bedroom occupies what is probably the best location in the entire residence, with its space divided almost equally between the very positive Life and Growth and Continuity sectors. The location of its bathroom is also good; not only is it in the Continuity sector, it is on the west side of the house, a good sector for anything related to water. Note that the bed has been positioned away from both sets of windows, in a yin sector of the room, and that a screen or room divider has been used to mask it from the knife-edge of the bedroom door, which is a little too close for comfort. It would be better if the bedroom door were not opposite one of the windows, but they do not line up directly on the same axis, so this is permissible.

Pages 28–29, 35, 38–39, 64, 78–80.

4) What is your analysis of the guest bedroom?

The guest bedroom is divided between a very positive sector, Healing, and a tricky one, the Five Ghosts. However, the positioning of the bed is excellent; entirely within the Healing sector, on a yin side of the room, screened from the entrance and its door by a short entryway, and not in direct line of sight from either of the windows. The

Pages 28-29, 35-36, 38-39, 84.

location of the bathroom, with its water associations, in the Healing sector and on the northwest side of the house, is another positive element that helps counterbalance the tricky Five Ghosts sector encroaching into this room. Bathrooms can literally help flush bad influences away. The person occupying this room will be fine—especially if he is a young boy or man who will also receive the extra benefit of the northeastern orientation of the main entrance.

5) *Give an overall Nine Stars reading of the main living and dining area.*

Pages 36-40.

The location of this key area is really quite poor. Although the Life and Growth, Continuity, and Heavenly Healing sectors govern parts of this space, the bulk of it is taken up by the unholy trinity of Disaster, Death, and Six Conflicts, the more or less neutral entrance, and the problematic Five Ghosts. In this poorly situated but very important living and dining area, we will have to use our knowledge and ingenuity to counter these negative influences and achieve maximum harmony and security for the people living here.

6) *Going back to the floor plan given in Figure 32, carefully study the placement of the furniture and accessories in the main living and dining area. Can you give a detailed explanation of the placement of these items?*

There are many ways to work at offsetting the influence of bad feng shui. The following are simply some suggestions for this particular space: you will probably be able to think of many other viable solutions. Use your imagination! If you remain faithful to the principles of feng shui we have introduced so far, you will be fine.

104

Let's start with the positioning of the major pieces of furniture. The dining room table is in an excellent location, entirely within the portion of the Healing sector that extends into this space. The sofa is also well-situated, with almost all of it falling into the Life and Growth sector. Both the sofa and the coffee table in front of it are circular forms, smooth and rounded. Such forms are good for calming and balancing the strong *yang* force given this space by the northeast entrance; they are also associated with water and are therefore good in their location along the west wall of the living and dining area. The goldfish bowl situated on a table along the west wall continues this watery theme and strengthens the small sliver of the Continuity sector that falls here. It is also important to note that the qi center of the space has been left open, airy, and unblocked.

Page 88 and Figure 27.

Page 63-64.

Although the position of the living room is not terribly good from the point of view of the Nine Stars analysis, the fact that its main windows face south is a fortunate bit of luck. The sunlight and warmth and other positive things associated with the Red Bird of the south will help offset or neutralize some of the influences from the Disaster and Death sectors.

Page 34.

Protection can further enhanced by the large potted plant or indoor tree placed as a screen in front of the southernmost window. This tree should also have a good-luck talisman tied to its trunk with red cords, along with two small red envelopes, each with three coins in them. The strong life force of the tree, supplemented by these tools of good fortune, will do much to stabilize bad influences coming into the house from the Disaster sector.

Pages 89-92, 96-99.

Two other items are also intended to modify the influences of the Disaster sector. The first is a large, warm-colored carpet. The one shown here is rectangular, but a circular one in warm beige or some other rich color would also do well here. Definitely avoid carpets in cool or cold colors in the Disaster, Death, or Six Conflicts sectors. The second item is something for the coffee table. It can be a good luck charm of your choosing—some favored figurine, statuette, or other curio—or it could be a vase of live flowers with water, to further enhance the water and growth themes we have already established in this area.

This brings us to the Death sector, the most troublesome and challenging area. It is located in the southeast corner of this particular space, which tones down its powerful influences a bit, but not enough. Here we might use a confrontational approach, placing a large standing cactus plant to stand as a thorny guardian at the juncture of the Disaster and Death sector. Another possibility would be to use a Seven Stars sword or Chinese coin sword. If you prefer a less militant approach, a religious image of the Buddha, Christ, or an angel might be placed here instead, or a text such as a Bible, Koran, or sutra book. This is also a place where a statue of a dragon, tiger, or lion could be used to good effect. It is up to you!

Pages 88-89, 92-94.

The Death sector is bad for major pieces of furniture, especially ones occupied by people for any length of time. But it is fine for closets, storage areas, bookshelves, and electronic equipment. Here, we have placed the TV, VCR, and stereo systems together in the Death sector. Note also the curtains on the window serving as a screen to bad influences trying to enter from this sector.

Pages 39-40.

We now move into the Six Conflicts sector. This is an uneasy sector, stabilized here by a warm-colored painting on the wall. The large standing floor lamp placed near the juncture with the Death sector also adds light and warmth to this area, and it might be a good idea to leave one of the bulbs on at night to soothe this troublesome spot. Note that the goldfish bowl on the opposite west wall will also provide some help, nourishing the qi in this area and calming down the Six Conflicts sector.

Pages 73-74, 88.

The sector containing the entrance itself is very important in its relation to the qi center and in determining the overall star matrix for a site. It also determines who will derive special benefit from living in a particular dwelling, and as we have already seen, the northeast entrance of this particular dwelling is of greatest benefit for a boy or young man. In this important sector, we have placed a set of display shelves right beside the entrance itself. A protective talisman from among the ones featured in this book should be placed on the top shelf. Some people might also like to hang a string of three, five, or seven Chinese coins tied with red cords above the top of the door-frame. The middle shelves can be a playground for small sculptures, figurines, or other antique objects for good luck—remember, their number is important. The lower shelves can be used for books.

Pages 65-70, 88-90, 96-99.

Finally, we come to the Five Ghosts sector. This is a tricky sector, and further complicated by a small window opening to the north, the domain of the Dark Warrior. The masking wall we set up to separate the entrance from the open kitchen also serves here to contain and stabilize troubling influences in this sector. The window itself should

Pages 32-33.

be curtained, as shown in the floor plan. In front of the window we have placed a table with a lamp on either end and a wooden *bagua* plaque in the center. The lamp nearest the window should be kept lit at night (you can use a low-watt bulb) to protect this area and drive away dark forces.

Pages 73-74, 92-93.

This concludes our final exercise. You now have a solid grasp of the fundamentals of feng shui analysis using the Nine Stars method, and a versatile kit of tools for modifying the feng shui of any space you choose to work with. Good feng shui arrangements do not have to be either costly or complicated. Remember that the secret of feng shui, as of life itself, is the balanced integration of the many forces—physical and spiritual—that shape your environment. So base yourself on the solid principles introduced here, but also let your own good sense and intuition be your guide. Open yourself to what your environment is telling you, and use what you have learned here to create a space for yourself that is as serene, comfortable, and nurturing as it can be. The world is a less threatening place with a happy, well-balanced home at the center of it. And sometimes, moving your furniture *can* change your life.

SOURCES

Abell, George. *Exploration of the Universe*. New York: Holt, Rhinehart, and Winston, 1969.

Bergland, Lars. *The Secrets of Luo Shu*. Lund, Sweden: Lund University, 1990.

Burkhardt, V.R. *Chinese Creeds and Customs*. 3 vols. Hong Kong: 1958.

Cheng, Te-kun. "Yin-yang Wu-hsiang in Han Art," *Harvard Journal of Asiatic Studies* (20), 1957.

Fung, Yu-lan. *A History of Chinese Philosophy*. 2 vols. Princeton University Press, 1952–53.

Hatchett, Clint. *The Glow in the Dark Night Sky*. New York: Random House, 1988.

Ho, Peng Yoke. "Li, Qi, and Shu: Magic Squares in East and West," *Papers on Far Eastern History* (8). Canberra, Australia: 1973.

Lip, Evelyn. *Feng Shui for the Home*. Torrance, California: Heian International, 1990.

Major, John S. "The Five Phases, Magic Squares, and Schematic Cosmology," in Henry Rosemont, Jr., ed., *Explorations in Early Chinese Cosmology*. Atlanta: The Scholars Press, 1984.

Merton, Merlina. *Feng Shui for Better Living*. Manila: Mervera, 1993.

Needham, Joseph. *Science and Civilization in China*. Vols. 3 and 4. Cambridge University Press, 1959.

English Texts

Walters, Derek. *Feng Shui Handbook*. San Francisco: Aquarian, 1991.

Rossbach, Sarah. *Living Color: Master Lin Yun's Guide to Feng Shui and the Art of Color*. New York: Kodansha International, 1994.

Williams, C.A.S. *Chinese Symbolism and Art Motives*. New York: The Julian Press, 1960.

Chinese Texts   Bai Yunshenren. *Dili fengshui jingyao* (Important Things in Geography and Feng Shui). Hong Kong: Da De, n.d.

Cai Yaoju. *Jili damende fangxiang* (Orientations for Lucky Entrances and Doorways). Taiwan: Yuk Zhi, n.d.

Chang Xiafuzi: *Yangzhai jicheng* (A Compilation on Yang Residences). Taipei: Wen Yuan Publishing, 1993.

Chen Lifu and Zhou Dingheng. *Zhouyi yingyongzhi yanjiushu* (Research on Applications of the Yijing), vol. 1. Taiwan: Chunghua, 1981.

Chen, Yongzheng. *Zhongguo fangshu dazidian* (Dictionary of Chinese Daoism). Guangdong: Zhongshan University Press / Xinhua Publishing, 1991.

Dao Zang. *Dao zang* (Daoist Treasures). 1487. Reprint, Taiwan: Yi Wen Yin Shu Guan, 1977.

Fang Chaoxuan. *Shilai fengshui jinji* (Forbidden Practices in Interior Feng Shui). Hong Kong: Qin Shi Yuan Publishing, 1994.

Huang Xiumin and Zhang Li. *Zhongguo shi daming dao* (The Ten Most Famous Daoist Priests in China). Jilin: Yanbian University Press / Xinhua Publishing, 1992.

Jiang Kanwen. *Xiandai jinzhu yu fengshui* (Contemporary Architecture and Feng Shui). Hong Kong: Qin Shi Yuan Publishing, 1993.

Lai, Zhide. *Yijing laizhu tujie* (The Yijing with Master Lai's Annotations and Illustrations). 1602. Reprint, Sichuan: Sichuan Book Company, 1988.

Wang Yude. *Gudai fengshui shuzhuping* (Annotated Study and Criticism on Ancient Feng Shui). Beijing: Beijing Teacher's College Press, 1992.

Wuguitang tongshu (Wuguitang Chinese Almanac). Canton: 1890.

Xu Xiang. *Fengshui rumen* (Feng Shui for Beginners). Hong Kong: Changjiang Publishing, n.d.

Yang Yifang. *Fengshui gejue* (Songs of Feng Shui). Hong Kong: Kuai Ze, n.d.

Yun Gizi. *Dili longxue panduan* (Locating Geographical Dragons and Meridians). Macao: New Enterprise Publishing, n.d..

Zhao Jinfeng. *Dili wujue* (The Five Songs of Geography). 1786. Reprint, Hong Kong: Chilin Publishing , n.d.

Zhao Jinxing. *Yinyang zhai daquan* (Complete Work on Yin-Yang Residences). Henan: Zhengzhou Antique Books Press, 1995.

ABOUT THE AUTHOR

Kwan Lau, born and raised in Hong Kong, is the descendant of a long line of divination and feng shui experts. He was trained as an architect in the United States, and holds an advanced degree in architectural acoustics. He is also an ordained lay Buddhist, a scholar of classical and modern Chinese literature, history, and the arts, and a connoisseur of Chinese antiques. He is the author of *The Secrets of Chinese Astrology* and *The I Ching Tarot*, also published by Tengu Books, and currently lives in New York City as a writer and artist.